Norway

Everything You Need
to Know

4

Introduction to Norway: Land of the Vikings

Nestled in the northern reaches of Europe, Norway emerges as a land of enchanting landscapes and captivating history. It's a place where nature's grandeur and the legacy of the formidable Vikings intertwine to create a country that is both awe-inspiring and culturally rich.

Situated in the Scandinavian Peninsula, Norway is renowned for its stunning fjords, vast glaciers, and pristine wilderness. Its rugged terrain, carved by ancient ice sheets, offers some of the most breathtaking vistas on Earth. From the towering cliffs of the Geirangerfjord to the serene beauty of the Hardangerfjord, Norway's fjords are unparalleled in their majesty.

But beyond its natural wonders, Norway's history is a tale that stretches back millennia. Perhaps most famously, it's the homeland of the Vikings, a seafaring people who once ruled the northern seas and left an indelible mark on European history. The word "Viking" conjures images of fearless warriors and skilled navigators, and rightly so. These Norsemen, who thrived between the 8th and 11th centuries, expanded their influence across Europe, Asia, and even North America, leaving behind a legacy that continues to captivate our imaginations.

The Viking Age is just one chapter in Norway's rich historical tapestry. Before the arrival of the Vikings, Norway's early inhabitants lived off the land, hunting and gathering in a harsh, unforgiving environment. As the centuries passed, they developed distinct cultural practices, such as the construction of the iconic stave churches, which still stand as testaments to their craftsmanship and faith.

Norway's history also includes periods of union with neighboring nations, notably Denmark and Sweden. These unions brought both prosperity and challenges, shaping the nation's identity and its enduring quest for independence.

In the 19th century, Norway embarked on a journey towards self-determination. It peacefully dissolved its union with Sweden in 1905, solidifying its status as a sovereign nation. Since then, Norway has blossomed into a thriving modern society, known for its commitment to social welfare, education, and environmental conservation.

As we delve deeper into this book, we'll explore Norway's geography, culture, cuisine, and the myriad ways it has evolved over the centuries. From the northern lights dancing in Arctic skies to the bustling streets of Oslo, Norway's story is one of resilience, innovation, and an unbreakable connection to its Viking heritage.

Norway's Geographic Diversity

Norway's geographic diversity is a testament to nature's boundless creativity. This Scandinavian jewel stretches across the northern reaches of Europe, boasting a landscape that is as diverse as it is breathtaking. From the windswept coasts to the towering mountains, and from the tranquil fjords to the frozen Arctic tundra, Norway's terrain is a captivating mosaic of natural wonders.

At its western edge, Norway is graced by the majestic Norwegian Sea, which opens up into the vast expanse of the North Atlantic Ocean. The rugged coastline, characterized by countless fjords and inlets, is a defining feature of the country's geography. Fjords like the iconic Geirangerfjord and Nærøyfjord cut deep into the land, their steep cliffs and crystal-clear waters creating dramatic and awe-inspiring vistas that draw visitors from around the world.

Venturing inland, Norway's topography changes dramatically. The backbone of the country is formed by the Scandinavian Mountains, or "fjell" in Norwegian. These mountains, which include the formidable Jotunheimen range, are some of the highest in Europe, with peaks soaring above 8,000 feet. Blanketed in snow and ice for much of the year, they provide a playground for winter sports enthusiasts and a challenge for mountaineers.

But Norway's geographic diversity doesn't stop at its fjords and mountains. In the far north, the Arctic Circle marks the boundary of the Arctic region, where the land gives way to the Arctic Ocean. Here, the polar night reigns in winter, with months of continuous darkness followed by the midnight sun in summer, when the sun never sets. It's a land of extremes, where reindeer roam and the northern lights dance across the night sky.

To the east, Norway shares a border with Sweden and Finland, and the landscape transitions into rolling hills and dense forests. The vast boreal forests of Norway are home to a rich variety of wildlife, including moose, wolves, lynx, and bears. The forests also provide a source of timber, contributing to Norway's economy and culture.

In the south, the climate is milder, and the landscape becomes more pastoral. Here, you'll find fertile farmland, picturesque villages, and the bustling city of Oslo, the capital of Norway. The southern coast is known for its archipelagos and coastal culture, where fishing and maritime traditions have deep roots.

Norway's geographic diversity isn't just a backdrop to its culture and history; it's woven into the fabric of the nation's identity. It shapes the lifestyle of its people, influences their industries, and offers endless opportunities for outdoor adventures. Whether you're drawn to the serene beauty of a fjord, the challenge of a mountain hike, or the magic of the Arctic, Norway's diverse geography has something to offer every traveler and explorer.

Early History of Norway: From Ice Age to Iron Age

The early history of Norway is a saga of resilience and adaptation, shaped by the forces of nature and the indomitable spirit of its early inhabitants. This journey through time takes us from the icy grip of the last Ice Age to the dawn of the Iron Age, a span of thousands of years during which Norway's landscape and people underwent profound transformations.

As the last Ice Age waned around 11,000 years ago, Norway began to emerge from the icy depths that had covered it for millennia. Glaciers receded, carving out the distinctive fjords that would later become some of Norway's most iconic features. The land was gradually colonized by plants, animals, and, eventually, humans.

The first human traces in Norway date back to around 9500 BCE when nomadic hunter-gatherer tribes ventured into the region. These early settlers relied on hunting, fishing, and foraging to sustain their communities, making use of the abundant natural resources offered by Norway's rugged terrain.

Over time, these scattered tribes began to form more organized societies. By 3000 BCE, the people of Norway had mastered agriculture, cultivating crops and domesticating animals. This transition to farming had a profound impact on their way of life, allowing for larger settlements, more stable food sources, and the development of more complex social structures.

Around 1500 BCE, Norway entered the Bronze Age, marked by the use of bronze tools and the construction of impressive burial mounds, some of which still dot the landscape today. This era saw the emergence of distinct regional cultures and trade networks, connecting Norway to neighboring regions in Scandinavia and beyond.

The transition from the Bronze Age to the Iron Age, around 500 BCE, brought further advancements. Ironworking became widespread, enabling the production of more durable tools and weapons. The Iron Age also saw the rise of chiefdoms and tribal societies, each with its own unique customs and traditions.

Throughout this period, contact with the outside world played a significant role in shaping Norway's culture. Trade routes extended across Europe, and Norway's rich natural resources, including timber and fish, made it an attractive destination for traders and explorers. This contact introduced new ideas, technologies, and goods to the region, influencing the development of its societies.

It's important to note that the history of early Norway is not a linear progression but a tapestry of various cultures, migrations, and influences. Different regions of Norway developed distinct identities, and the path to a unified nation was long and complex.

Viking Age in Norway: Raiders and Explorers

The Viking Age in Norway represents one of the most captivating and enigmatic periods in the nation's history. Spanning from the late 8th century to the 11th century, this era witnessed the emergence of the Vikings, a seafaring people whose impact reached far beyond their homeland.

The word "Viking" itself has become synonymous with adventure and exploration, and rightly so. These intrepid Norsemen hailed from the rugged coastlines, fjords, and islands of Norway, and they embarked on journeys that would shape the course of history.

At the heart of the Viking Age was a quest for adventure and riches. The Vikings were skilled navigators who built sturdy longships capable of crossing vast stretches of ocean. With these vessels, they ventured across the North Atlantic to reach as far as Iceland, Greenland, and even North America, centuries before Columbus set foot in the New World.

But the Vikings were not mere explorers; they were also fearsome raiders. In their dragon-headed longships, they raided coastal communities throughout Europe, from the British Isles to the Mediterranean. The Viking raids struck terror into the hearts of those they encountered, earning them a reputation as formidable warriors.

One of the most famous Viking leaders to emerge from Norway was the legendary Ragnar Lothbrok, whose exploits have been celebrated in sagas and legends. These stories often blend history with myth, making it challenging to separate fact from fiction. Still, the deeds of Ragnar and other Viking chieftains left an indelible mark on the historical record.

While the Vikings are often associated with plunder and pillage, they were also traders and settlers. They established trading routes that connected the Baltic Sea with the Middle East, facilitating the exchange of goods and ideas. Vikings settled in various regions they visited, such as the Danelaw in England and Normandy in France, leaving lasting cultural influences in their wake.

Norway itself was not a unified kingdom during the Viking Age. Instead, it was divided into several chieftaincies, each ruled by a local chief or jarl. These chieftains often vied for power and territory, and their rivalries sometimes fueled Viking expeditions.

The Viking Age eventually gave way to a period of consolidation and Christianization. By the 11th century, Norway began to coalesce into a more centralized kingdom under the rule of King Olaf II (St. Olav), who played a pivotal role in the conversion of Norway to Christianity.

Medieval Norway: Kingdoms and Dynasties

The medieval period in Norway, spanning from the 11th to the 16th century, marked a significant chapter in the nation's history. During this time, Norway evolved from a collection of disparate chieftaincies into a more centralized monarchy, witnessed the emergence of powerful dynasties, and navigated through periods of both prosperity and adversity.

At the onset of the medieval era, Norway was a patchwork of regional chieftaincies, each ruled by a local chief or jarl. The Viking Age had given way to a more settled way of life, and the influence of Christianity continued to grow. It was during this period that King Olaf II, known as St. Olav, ascended to the throne and played a pivotal role in the Christianization of Norway. His reign marked the beginning of efforts to unite the country under a single faith.

Following St. Olav's death, Norway experienced a period of political turmoil as various chieftains and factions vied for control. The kingdom was divided into smaller territories ruled by different dynasties, including the Gille dynasty, the Sverre dynasty, and the Bagler dynasty, each leaving its mark on Norway's medieval history.

One of the most notable rulers of this period was King Haakon IV, who ascended to the throne in the early 13th century. His reign saw the consolidation of royal power and the strengthening of the monarchy. He introduced administrative reforms, improved the legal system, and laid the groundwork for a more centralized government. His rule also witnessed conflicts with neighboring nations, including a series of wars with Scotland.

In the 14th century, Norway experienced a series of challenges, including the Black Death, which ravaged the population, and political instability. The country faced power struggles and changing alliances as it navigated through these difficult times.

One of the most significant events in medieval Norway was the Kalmar Union in the late 14th century, which saw Norway united with Denmark and Sweden under a single monarch. While this union brought about a degree of stability, it also diminished Norway's independence as a separate kingdom.

Throughout the medieval period, Norway's monarchy continued to evolve, and the country gradually transitioned into the Late Middle Ages. The dynastic struggles, union with Denmark, and economic challenges shapcd the nation's identity and institutions. Despite these complexities, Norway remained a vibrant and culturally rich land with a strong connection to its Viking heritage.

Union with Denmark: Norway's Dark Ages

The union between Norway and Denmark, which endured for over four centuries, is often referred to as Norway's "Dark Ages." This period, which began in the late 14th century and lasted until the early 19th century, was marked by significant political and cultural changes, as Norway found itself under the rule of the Danish crown.

The union with Denmark came about as a result of the Kalmar Union, which united Denmark, Norway, and Sweden under a single monarch. It was established in 1397 and initially intended to provide a measure of stability in the face of external threats, particularly from the Hanseatic League and the power struggles in Europe.

For Norway, this union had profound consequences. The Norwegian monarchy and its institutions were gradually assimilated into the Danish kingdom, eroding the country's autonomy. The Danish king appointed governors, known as "Lensmenn," to administer the various regions of Norway, and the country effectively became a subordinate province.

During this period, Norway's political influence waned, and its economy was increasingly controlled by the Hanseatic League, a powerful trading network. The League established a firm foothold in Norwegian cities such as Bergen and Trondheim, exerting considerable economic dominance over the region. While these cities prospered, much of the Norwegian countryside struggled under the weight of heavy taxation and economic exploitation.

The union with Denmark also saw the decline of the Norwegian language as a language of administration and culture. Danish became the official language of government and education, and the use of Norwegian dialects was discouraged. This linguistic shift had a lasting impact on the development of the Norwegian language.

Despite the challenges and hardships faced during this period, Norway managed to preserve elements of its cultural identity. Folk traditions, music, and local customs persisted in rural communities, serving as a reminder of Norway's rich heritage. However, the dominance of Danish influence in the urban centers and at the highest levels of government was undeniable.

The Union with Denmark persisted until 1814 when a series of events, including the Napoleonic Wars, led to the dissolution of the union. At the Treaty of Kiel in 1814, Norway was ceded to the King of Sweden, sparking a short-lived period of Swedish rule. However, the people of Norway, inspired by a growing sense of national identity, rejected Swedish rule and drafted their own constitution on May 17, 1814, which laid the foundation for the modern Norwegian state.

While the union with Denmark represents a challenging and, in many ways, a dark period in Norway's history, it also played a role in shaping the nation's identity and fostering a spirit of resilience and determination that would guide Norway into a new era of independence and self-determination.

The Road to Independence: 19th-Century Norway

The 19th century marked a pivotal period in Norway's history as the nation embarked on a journey towards independence and self-determination. After centuries of foreign rule and union with Denmark and then Sweden, the people of Norway began to assert their national identity and work towards establishing their own sovereign state.

The seeds of Norway's quest for independence were sown in the early 19th century. In 1814, following the Napoleonic Wars and the Treaty of Kiel, Norway was ceded to Sweden after over four centuries of union with Denmark. However, the people of Norway were not content with this arrangement, and they saw an opportunity to chart their own destiny.

In a remarkable display of unity, delegates from across Norway gathered at Eidsvoll in the spring of 1814 to draft a constitution for the nation. The resulting Eidsvoll Constitution, adopted on May 17, 1814, laid the foundation for a modern, independent Norway. This date is celebrated annually as Norway's Constitution Day, a symbol of the nation's commitment to its newfound democratic ideals.

Despite this bold step towards nationhood, Norway's path to independence was not without its challenges. Sweden was reluctant to grant Norway full autonomy, and a brief war known as the Swedish-Norwegian War of 1814 ensued. The conflict ultimately led to the Convention of

Moss in August 1814, where the terms of the union between Norway and Sweden were established.

Under the terms of the union, Norway retained its own constitution, legal system, and parliament, known as the Storting. However, foreign affairs and defense were under Swedish control, and there was a sense of unease about the limitations on Norwegian sovereignty.

Throughout the 19th century, Norway's political landscape was marked by efforts to secure greater independence from Sweden. The Norwegian independence movement gained momentum, and political leaders, such as Henrik Wergeland and Bjørnstjerne Bjørnson, played instrumental roles in advocating for Norwegian nationalism.

In 1905, after years of negotiations and political maneuvering, Norway peacefully dissolved the union with Sweden. On June 7, 1905, the Norwegian parliament, the Storting, declared the union null and void, effectively asserting Norway's independence. Prince Carl of Denmark was subsequently elected as King Haakon VII of Norway, and a new era of Norwegian sovereignty began.

Modern Norway: A Thriving Nation

In the wake of its hard-fought journey to independence in the early 20th century, Norway emerged as a nation characterized by resilience, progress, and a commitment to social welfare. The modern era in Norway has seen remarkable developments across various facets of its society, transforming it into a thriving and prosperous nation.

One of the defining features of modern Norway is its robust economy. Rich in natural resources, including oil, gas, and hydropower, Norway has managed its wealth wisely. The discovery of North Sea oil in the 1960s ushered in an era of economic prosperity, leading to the creation of the Government Pension Fund Global, often referred to as the Norwegian Sovereign Wealth Fund. This fund has become one of the largest in the world, providing financial security and stability for the country's future generations.

Norway's economy isn't solely reliant on oil and gas, though. The nation boasts a diverse range of industries, including shipbuilding, maritime technology, telecommunications, and pharmaceuticals. Its strong focus on innovation and technology has made it a global leader in sectors such as renewable energy and green technology.

Beyond its economic prowess, Norway is renowned for its commitment to social welfare. The Norwegian welfare state, characterized by a comprehensive healthcare system, accessible education, and a strong safety net, ensures that citizens enjoy a high standard of living and a sense of security. Universal healthcare is available to all residents, and education, from preschool to university, is largely funded by the state, making it accessible to everyone.

Norway's dedication to environmental sustainability is another hallmark of its modern identity. The country has embraced renewable energy sources, particularly hydropower, as a clean and abundant source of electricity. Norway's stunning fjords and wilderness areas are carefully preserved, and stringent environmental regulations ensure the protection of its natural beauty.

Culturally, Norway continues to celebrate its rich heritage while embracing modern influences. The nation has produced internationally acclaimed artists, authors, musicians, and designers, contributing to a vibrant cultural scene. The works of playwright Henrik Ibsen and painter Edvard Munch, as well as the contemporary music of artists like Kygo and Sigrid, have all left their mark on the global stage.

In terms of foreign policy, Norway maintains a reputation as a promoter of peace and diplomacy. The nation has been actively engaged in international conflict resolution efforts and humanitarian aid. It is also a member of various international organizations, including the United Nations and NATO.

In recent years, Norway has faced global challenges such as climate change, immigration, and the ongoing quest for social equality. However, its proactive approach to addressing these issues underscores its commitment to maintaining a progressive and inclusive society.

Norse Mythology: Legends and Gods

Norse mythology is a rich tapestry of legends, gods, and cosmic narratives that have fascinated and captivated generations of readers and scholars. Rooted in the oral traditions of the ancient Germanic peoples, Norse mythology offers a window into the worldviews, beliefs, and values of the early Norse societies, particularly those of the Vikings who hailed from what is now modern-day Scandinavia.

At the heart of Norse mythology are the Aesir and the Vanir, two groups of deities who are central to the Norse pantheon. The Aesir, led by Odin, the Allfather, are associated with war, wisdom, and rulership. Odin, often depicted as a wise old man with a long beard and one eye, is the chief of the Aesir and the god of knowledge and poetry. His relentless quest for wisdom led him to sacrifice an eye at the Well of Mímir in exchange for knowledge.

Thor, the mighty god of thunder, is another prominent member of the Aesir. He wields the powerful hammer, Mjölnir, and is a protector of both gods and humans. His strength and bravery are celebrated in numerous tales, as he battles giants and monsters to defend the realms.

The Vanir, on the other hand, are associated with fertility, nature, and prosperity. Freyja, the goddess of love and fertility, is one of the most revered Vanir deities. Her brother Freyr is the god of agriculture and prosperity. Both Freyja and Freyr are associated with the bountiful harvest and the beauty of nature. The interplay between the Aesir and the Vanir is a recurring theme in Norse mythology.

They once waged war against each other but eventually made peace, exchanging hostages to maintain harmony. This integration of two divine families reflects the importance of balance in Norse cosmology.

The cosmos of Norse mythology consists of nine realms, interconnected by the great cosmic tree, Yggdrasil. These realms include Asgard, the realm of the Aesir; Midgard, the world of humans; and Jotunheim, the land of giants. Each realm is inhabited by various beings and creatures, contributing to the rich tapestry of Norse legends.

One of the most iconic elements of Norse mythology is the concept of Ragnarök, the apocalyptic event that foretells the end of the world and the ultimate destruction of the gods. This cataclysmic battle is prophesied to involve fierce conflicts between gods, giants, and monsters, resulting in the world being submerged in water and reborn anew.

The Norse mythological narratives are not only filled with epic battles and cosmic struggles but also explore themes of fate, honor, and the cyclical nature of existence. They were passed down through oral tradition until they were eventually recorded in written texts like the Poetic Edda and the Prose Edda in the 13th century, preserving these timeless stories for generations to come.

Norse mythology continues to be a source of inspiration in literature, art, and popular culture, and its gods and legends continue to capture the imagination of people worldwide. It's a testament to the enduring power of these ancient tales that they remain a vibrant part of our cultural heritage, inviting us to explore the mysteries of the Viking cosmos and the rich tapestry of Norse mythology.

The Sami People: Indigenous Culture

The Sami people, often referred to as the Sámi or Saami, are the indigenous inhabitants of Sápmi, a region that stretches across the northern parts of Norway, Sweden, Finland, and Russia's Kola Peninsula. With a rich and enduring cultural heritage that spans thousands of years, the Sami have a unique and vibrant way of life that is deeply intertwined with the natural world of the Arctic North.

The history of the Sami people is a testament to their resilience and adaptability. Archaeological evidence suggests that the Sami have inhabited the Arctic region for at least 4,000 years, making them one of Europe's oldest indigenous cultures. Throughout their history, the Sami have faced numerous challenges, including external pressures from neighboring societies and governments. However, they have maintained their distinct cultural identity, language, and way of life.

One of the most defining aspects of Sami culture is their connection to the land and their traditional livelihoods. Traditionally, the Sami were nomadic herders, primarily relying on reindeer husbandry for sustenance and trade. The reindeer herds provided meat, hides, and antlers, which were used for food, clothing, and tools. This semi-nomadic lifestyle allowed the Sami to move with the changing seasons, following the migratory patterns of the reindeer.

The Sami language, known as Sámi or Sami, is a group of closely related Uralic languages with several dialects. Each dialect is associated with a specific region and has its own unique characteristics. The preservation of the Sami language has been a crucial aspect of maintaining their cultural identity, and efforts to revitalize and promote the language continue today.

Traditional Sami clothing is both functional and culturally significant. The iconic gákti, a brightly colored traditional outfit, varies in design and color patterns among different Sami groups and regions. These garments are not only beautiful but also well-suited to the harsh Arctic climate, providing warmth and protection.

Sami culture is rich in storytelling and oral traditions. Their stories, legends, and yoiks (a form of traditional song) are important vehicles for passing down knowledge, values, and history from one generation to the next. These narratives often feature themes related to nature, animals, and the spirit world.

Religion and spirituality have also played a significant role in Sami culture. Traditionally, the Sami practiced animism, believing that all natural elements possessed spirits. They conducted rituals to maintain harmony with the spirits and ensure the well-being of their communities. Over time, the introduction of Christianity influenced some aspects of Sami spirituality, leading to a blend of traditional and Christian beliefs.

The Sami people have not been immune to the challenges faced by many indigenous communities worldwide. Historical periods of forced assimilation, discrimination, and land dispossession have left lasting scars. However, in recent decades, there has been a resurgence of Sami cultural pride and activism, leading to increased recognition of their rights and the protection of their lands and traditions.

Today, the Sami people continue to navigate the complexities of preserving their ancient culture while adapting to the modern world. They are active participants in contemporary society, contributing to politics, arts, and academia, all while safeguarding their unique identity and the legacy of their ancestors. The story of the Sami people is one of resilience, cultural richness, and a deep connection to the Arctic lands they call home.

Norwegian Wildlife: A Natural Wonderland

Norway's pristine landscapes, from its rugged mountains to its tranquil fjords, are not only breathtaking but also teeming with diverse wildlife. The country's natural wonders provide a habitat for a wide array of species, making it a true haven for nature enthusiasts and wildlife lovers.

The king of Norway's wilderness is undoubtedly the mighty moose, known locally as the "elg." These imposing creatures, with their massive antlers, are a common sight in Norway's forests and woodlands. They are the largest species of deer in Europe and have adapted well to the country's varied terrain.

In addition to moose, Norway is also home to several other species of deer, including roe deer and reindeer. The reindeer, or "rein," have a special place in Sami culture and are herded by the indigenous Sami people, primarily in the northern reaches of Norway.

The country's coastline and fjords offer prime habitat for a diverse range of marine life. Whales, including orcas, humpback whales, and minke whales, are commonly spotted in Norwegian waters. Whale-watching tours are a popular activity for tourists seeking to witness these majestic creatures in their natural environment. Norway's birdlife is equally impressive, with numerous species of seabirds, waterfowl, and raptors inhabiting the country. Puffins, with their distinctive orange bills, are often seen on

Norway's coastal cliffs. Eagles, including the iconic white-tailed eagle, soar above the fjords in search of prey.

The country's interior is home to a variety of smaller mammals, such as red foxes, Arctic foxes, and the elusive lynx. The lynx, known as the "gaupe" in Norwegian, is a solitary and elusive predator that roams the remote forests of Norway.

Norway's rivers and lakes are rich in fish, including salmon and trout. Anglers from around the world are drawn to Norway's pristine waters for the chance to catch these prized species. The country's strict conservation measures ensure the sustainability of its fisheries.

Perhaps one of the most iconic species associated with Norway is the polar bear. While polar bears are more commonly associated with the Arctic regions of Svalbard and the far north, they are a symbol of Norway's connection to the icy realms of the north.

The protection and conservation of wildlife are central to Norway's environmental policies. The country has established a network of national parks and nature reserves to safeguard its natural treasures. Efforts to protect endangered species and preserve critical habitats are ongoing, reflecting Norway's commitment to responsible stewardship of its natural world.

Exploring Norway's wild landscapes and encountering its diverse wildlife is a thrilling and enriching experience. From the majestic moose to the graceful reindeer, from the awe-inspiring whales to the charming puffins, Norway's natural wonderland offers a unique opportunity to connect with the beauty and diversity of the natural world.

Norwegian Cuisine: From Salmon to Koldtbord

Norwegian cuisine reflects the country's diverse and often rugged landscape, drawing inspiration from its abundant natural resources and traditional culinary practices. From the bounty of its cold, clear waters to the hearty dishes born of long winters, Norwegian food tells a story of adaptation and innovation.

One of Norway's culinary treasures is its salmon. Norwegian salmon is renowned worldwide for its quality and flavor. The cold, clean waters of Norway's fjords provide the perfect environment for salmon farming. Whether served smoked, gravlax-style, or simply grilled, Norwegian salmon is a delicacy that graces tables across the globe.

Another beloved seafood in Norway is the humble shrimp, often enjoyed fresh and cold, accompanied by a dollop of mayonnaise and a slice of lemon. Shrimp cocktail, or "reker" in Norwegian, is a classic appetizer enjoyed during summer months.

Norway's coastline and fjords offer a bounty of fish, including cod, haddock, and mackerel. Stockfish, a dried and preserved cod, has been a staple of the Norwegian diet for centuries. It's rehydrated and used in traditional dishes like bacalao, a hearty fish stew. Lutefisk, a dish made from dried fish (usually cod or ling), is another Norwegian specialty. The fish is rehydrated and treated with lye, then cooked and served with a variety of accompaniments, such as potatoes, bacon, and mustard sauce. It's a polarizing dish; some love it, while others find its unique texture and flavor an acquired taste. Norwegian cuisine also embraces hearty meats to sustain through the long, cold winters. Reindeer, often associated with the indigenous Sami culture, is a lean and tender meat enjoyed in dishes like "finnbiff" (reindeer stew). Another traditional meat dish is "lapskaus," a hearty stew typically made with beef or lamb, potatoes, and root vegetables.

Foraging is a cherished tradition in Norway, with people picking wild berries and mushrooms in the forests and mountains. Lingonberries and cloudberries are commonly used in jams and desserts, while chanterelles and porcini mushrooms find their way into savory dishes.

Bread is a fundamental part of Norwegian meals, and the country boasts a rich variety of bread types. "Flatbrød," a thin, crispbread, is a staple, often served with cheese, butter, or smoked salmon. "Lefse," a soft potato flatbread, is another popular choice, often enjoyed with sweet toppings like sugar and cinnamon.

No discussion of Norwegian cuisine would be complete without mentioning the koldtbord, a traditional Norwegian buffet. The koldtbord features an array of cold and hot dishes, including herring, cured meats, salads, and cheeses. It's a communal dining experience that allows guests to sample a wide range of flavors and specialties.

Norwegian sweets and desserts include classics like "kransekake," an almond ring cake often served at weddings and special occasions, and "riskrem," a creamy rice pudding topped with red berry sauce, enjoyed during Christmas festivities.

Scandinavian Design: Functionality and Beauty

Scandinavian design, often hailed as a pinnacle of minimalist elegance and functionality, has left an indelible mark on the world of interior design, architecture, and everyday living. Rooted in the countries of Denmark, Sweden, Norway, Finland, and Iceland, Scandinavian design is characterized by its emphasis on simplicity, clean lines, and the harmonious integration of form and function.

The origins of Scandinavian design can be traced back to the early 20th century, a time when the design world was dominated by ornate and elaborate styles. In contrast, Scandinavian designers sought to create objects and spaces that celebrated the beauty of simplicity and practicality.

One of the key principles of Scandinavian design is the idea that good design should improve people's lives. This emphasis on functionality is evident in the furniture and products that emerged from this design movement. Iconic pieces like the "Wishbone Chair" by Hans Wegner, the "Egg Chair" by Arne Jacobsen, and the "Paimio Chair" by Alvar Aalto exemplify the blend of form and function that defines Scandinavian design. These pieces are not only visually appealing but also comfortable and functional, embodying the belief that everyday objects should be a pleasure to use.

Natural materials play a significant role in Scandinavian design. Wood, in particular, is a favored material due to its warmth, versatility, and sustainability. Scandinavian designers have a deep appreciation for the beauty of wood grains and often leave surfaces untreated to showcase their natural character. This reverence for nature extends to other materials as well, with textiles, ceramics, and glass all being used to create pieces that bring a sense of the outdoors into interior spaces.

Light is another essential element in Scandinavian design, given the long, dark winters in the region. Designers like Poul Henningsen pioneered innovative lighting solutions that provide warm and diffused illumination. The iconic "PH Artichoke Lamp" is a prime example of how lighting can be both functional and visually striking.

Color palettes in Scandinavian design tend to be muted and neutral, with white, gray, and earthy tones dominating interiors. These colors create a sense of tranquility and lightness while allowing natural materials and textures to take center stage. Accents of color are sparingly used to add vibrancy and contrast.

Scandinavian design is not limited to furniture and decor; it extends to architecture and urban planning as well. Scandinavian cities are known for their functional and sustainable urban design, with an emphasis on pedestrian-friendly streets, green spaces, and efficient public transportation systems.

The enduring appeal of Scandinavian design lies in its timeless quality. It transcends trends and fads, remaining relevant and sought after across the globe. It's a design philosophy that marries form and function, beauty and practicality, simplicity and sophistication.

In the modern world, where clutter and complexity often overwhelm our lives, Scandinavian design serves as a reminder that less can indeed be more. It encourages us to surround ourselves with objects and spaces that bring joy, comfort, and a sense of tranquility. It's a celebration of the essential and a testament to the enduring power of good design.

The Northern Lights: Norway's Celestial Phenomenon

In the northern reaches of Norway, under the vast expanse of Arctic skies, one of the most enchanting natural wonders unfolds—the Northern Lights, also known as the Aurora Borealis. This celestial phenomenon has been captivating humanity for centuries, and Norway offers some of the most spectacular viewing opportunities on Earth.

The Northern Lights are a breathtaking display of colorful lights that dance across the night sky. They come in a variety of hues, including shades of green, pink, purple, and even red. This celestial spectacle is caused by the interaction between charged particles from the Sun and the Earth's magnetic field.

The journey of these charged particles begins millions of miles away on the Sun's surface. Solar storms and flares release vast amounts of charged particles, mainly electrons and protons, into space. Some of these particles are carried toward the Earth by the solar wind, a stream of charged particles constantly blowing from the Sun.

When these solar particles reach the Earth's magnetic field, they interact with the gases in our atmosphere, primarily oxygen and nitrogen. This interaction energizes the gases, causing them to emit light. The specific colors observed in the Northern Lights depend on the type of gas and the altitude at which the interaction occurs.

Norway's geographical location, with its proximity to the Arctic Circle, makes it one of the prime locations for Northern Lights viewing. The regions of Tromsø, Lofoten, and

Finnmark in northern Norway are particularly renowned for their clear skies and frequent Aurora displays.

Visitors flock to these northern regions, especially during the winter months when the nights are longest and the skies darkest. The combination of crisp, cold air and minimal light pollution creates an ideal environment for witnessing the Northern Lights in all their glory.

Chasing the Northern Lights has become a popular tourist activity in Norway, with tour operators offering a range of experiences, from Northern Lights safaris on snowmobiles to cozy evenings in heated glass igloos designed for optimal viewing. Travelers often find themselves bundled up in warm clothing, gazing upward in eager anticipation, waiting for the ethereal curtains of light to appear.

The best time to see the Northern Lights in Norway is generally from late September to early April, when the Arctic nights are at their longest. However, the Aurora is a fickle mistress, and clear skies and solar activity play significant roles in determining when and where it will make its appearance.

The Northern Lights hold deep cultural and historical significance in Norway, intertwined with ancient myths and legends. The indigenous Sami people believed that the lights were the spirits of their ancestors, while Norse mythology spoke of the lights as the Bifrost Bridge, a celestial path between the mortal realm and the gods.

Today, the Northern Lights continue to inspire wonder and awe, drawing travelers from around the world to witness this celestial ballet. It's a reminder of the profound beauty and mystery that the natural world can offer, a testament to the enduring allure of Norway's celestial phenomenon.

Fjords of Norway: Nature's Masterpieces

Norway's fjords are nothing short of nature's masterpieces, a breathtaking showcase of the Earth's geological and glacial artistry. These majestic, deep-cut valleys, carved over millennia, define Norway's dramatic coastal landscapes and stand as a testament to the enduring forces of nature.

So, what exactly is a fjord? A fjord is a long, narrow inlet of the sea, bordered by steep cliffs or mountains, typically formed by the submergence of a glaciated valley. Norway is renowned for its fjords, and they are an integral part of the country's identity and natural beauty.

The formation of fjords is a geological saga that spans thousands of years. It begins with the slow advance of glaciers during ice ages, which scoured and shaped the landscape. As glaciers flowed and eroded, they carved deep valleys into the existing terrain. These valleys then filled with seawater as sea levels rose, creating the unique and iconic fjords that we see today.

One of the most famous and striking fjords in Norway is the Geirangerfjord, a UNESCO World Heritage Site known for its awe-inspiring beauty. Its narrow, winding waters are flanked by towering cliffs, cascading waterfalls, and lush green forests. Cruising through the Geirangerfjord offers a front-row seat to nature's grandeur.

The Nærøyfjord, another UNESCO World Heritage Site, is celebrated for its narrowness and pristine wilderness. Its serpentine path is hemmed in by steep mountainsides, creating a sense of intimacy with the natural world.

Then there's the Sognefjord, the longest fjord in Norway and one of the longest in the world. This vast waterway stretches for 127 miles (205 kilometers) and boasts a remarkable diversity of landscapes, from serene villages to rugged cliffs.

These fjords are not just visually stunning; they also harbor unique ecosystems. The mix of saltwater and freshwater creates a fertile environment where marine life thrives. You can spot seals, porpoises, and a variety of fish in these nutrient-rich waters.

The fjords' dramatic landscapes have not only been a source of inspiration for artists, writers, and explorers throughout history but have also served as vital transportation routes for the people who call these regions home. Many fjord communities are nestled along the shoreline, and their picturesque villages, with colorful houses and rich cultural traditions, add to the charm of these natural wonders.

Outdoor enthusiasts flock to the fjords for adventure and recreation. Hiking trails offer breathtaking views from elevated vantage points, while kayaking and boat tours allow visitors to explore the fjords up close.

In winter, the fjords take on a different kind of magic. Snow-covered peaks and frozen waterfalls create a serene, almost otherworldly atmosphere. The Northern Lights often grace the skies above the fjords, adding an extra layer of wonder to the experience.

The fjords of Norway are a living testament to the geological and glacial forces that have shaped our planet. They are not just geological features but living, breathing ecosystems that continue to captivate and inspire all who have the privilege of witnessing their grandeur. Norway's fjords are nature's masterpieces, an enduring legacy of Earth's creative forces.

Oslo: The Vibrant Capital

Nestled along the shores of the Oslofjord, Norway's capital city, Oslo, is a vibrant and modern metropolis that seamlessly blends rich historical heritage with contemporary innovation. As you step into this dynamic city, you'll find yourself immersed in a world where urban sophistication coexists harmoniously with the serenity of nature.

Oslo's history can be traced back over a thousand years. Founded in the year 1040, it has grown from a small Viking settlement known as "Ánslo" into a thriving European capital. The city's name evolved over the centuries, eventually becoming Oslo in the early 20th century.

The Royal Palace, perched atop a gentle rise, is an iconic landmark that has been the residence of the Norwegian monarchs since its completion in 1849. Its neoclassical architecture and beautifully manicured gardens make it a must-visit attraction, and you can witness the Changing of the Guard ceremony that takes place daily during the summer months.

Karl Johans Gate, the city's main boulevard, stretches from the Royal Palace to the Central Station and is the pulse of Oslo's urban life. Lined with shops, restaurants, and historic buildings, it's a bustling thoroughfare where locals and visitors alike gather to stroll, shop, and dine.

Oslo's waterfront is a striking blend of modern architecture and maritime charm. The Oslo Opera House, a contemporary masterpiece that seems to rise from the fjord, invites exploration both inside and out. Its sloping roof is designed to allow visitors to walk up to its apex, providing panoramic views of the city and the fjord.

Another architectural gem is the Astrup Fearnley Museum of Modern Art, designed by the renowned architect Renzo Piano. The museum's distinctive design and world-class collection of contemporary art make it a cultural focal point.

Oslo's rich cultural tapestry extends to its museums and galleries. The Viking Ship Museum houses remarkably well-preserved Viking vessels, offering a glimpse into Norway's seafaring heritage. The Munch Museum showcases the works of the iconic Norwegian artist Edvard Munch, including his famous painting "The Scream."

Green spaces and natural beauty are integral to Oslo's identity. The Vigeland Park, with its collection of Gustav Vigeland's sculptures, is a serene oasis within the city, while the Oslo Botanical Garden provides a tranquil retreat for plant enthusiasts.

The city's culinary scene has blossomed in recent years, with a focus on locally sourced, high-quality ingredients. Seafood, especially salmon and cod, features prominently on menus, and traditional dishes like "rømmegrøt" (sour cream porridge) and "lutefisk" (dried fish) are enjoyed alongside modern Scandinavian cuisine.

Oslo's commitment to sustainability and eco-friendliness is evident in its public transportation system, which includes trams, buses, and ferries, all powered by renewable energy sources. The city's dedication to environmental responsibility aligns with Norway's broader efforts to combat climate change.

As the capital and largest city of Norway, Oslo is a thriving hub of business, culture, and innovation. Its vibrant neighborhoods, bustling markets, and cultural institutions cater to a diverse array of interests. From the historic district of Gamlebyen to the trendy neighborhoods of Grünerløkka and Vulkan, Oslo's neighborhoods offer distinct flavors and atmospheres.

The soul of Oslo is not confined to its city limits; it extends to the surrounding fjords, forests, and islands. The city's residents embrace the outdoors with enthusiasm, making hiking, skiing, and sailing integral parts of their lives.

Oslo, the vibrant capital of Norway, is a city that honors its history while embracing a progressive and sustainable future. It's a place where urban life meets the tranquility of nature, where innovation thrives alongside tradition, and where the warmth of its people welcomes all who visit. In Oslo, you'll discover a dynamic city with a timeless spirit, a place where the past and present harmoniously coexist in every corner and along every fjord.

Bergen: Hanseatic Heritage

Nestled along the southwestern coast of Norway, Bergen stands as a living testament to its rich Hanseatic heritage. This enchanting city, with its colorful historic buildings, bustling harbor, and vibrant cultural scene, is a window into the past, offering a glimpse into a bygone era when Bergen was a key trading hub of the Hanseatic League.

The story of Bergen's Hanseatic heritage is intertwined with its strategic location. Founded in 1070, Bergen quickly established itself as a vital trading post. Its sheltered harbor and proximity to the North Sea made it an ideal gateway for merchants and seafarers from across Europe, including those from the Hanseatic League.

The Hanseatic League, a powerful alliance of merchant guilds and towns, dominated trade in Northern Europe during the Middle Ages. Bergen, with its wealth of fish and timber, was a sought-after destination for the Hanseatic merchants. In 1360, the League established the Hanseatic Kontor in Bergen, a trading post and administrative center that would become an enduring symbol of their presence in the city.

Bryggen, the iconic wharf of Bergen, is perhaps the most tangible legacy of the Hanseatic period. These historic wooden buildings, with their distinctive gabled facades, line the waterfront and are a UNESCO World Heritage Site. Bryggen's enduring charm has made it a beloved symbol of Bergen's Hanseatic past.

Life in Bryggen during the Hanseatic era was far from glamorous. The merchants, known as "Hanseatics," lived and worked in close quarters in the wooden buildings. They engaged in trade, primarily dried fish, fish oil, and timber, which were highly sought-after commodities in Europe at the time.

Despite the challenging living conditions, the Hanseatics left an indelible mark on Bergen's culture and commerce. The legacy of their trading practices can still be seen in the city's bustling fish market, which has been a focal point of Bergen's trade for centuries.

The Hanseatic Museum, located in one of Bryggen's historic buildings, provides an immersive experience into the daily life of the Hanseatics. Visitors can explore the reconstructed living quarters, see artifacts from the era, and gain insight into the challenges and triumphs of these medieval merchants.

As Bergen evolved over the centuries, its Hanseatic heritage remained a cornerstone of its identity. The city's commitment to preserving its historic district, including Bryggen, ensures that the legacy of the Hanseatics remains a vibrant part of contemporary Bergen.

Today, Bergen is a thriving city with a diverse cultural scene, a lively arts community, and a deep appreciation for its maritime history. Visitors can explore its charming neighborhoods, visit its museums and galleries, and savor its culinary delights, including fresh seafood and traditional Norwegian dishes.

Bergen's annual Hanseatic Days, a lively cultural festival, celebrates the city's Hanseatic heritage with music, dance, and historical reenactments. It's a testament to the enduring influence of the Hanseatics on the city's culture and traditions.

Bergen's Hanseatic heritage is not just a chapter in its history but a living, breathing part of its identity. The echoes of the Hanseatic era can be heard in the creaking wooden planks of Bryggen, felt in the vibrant energy of its streets, and seen in the proud smiles of its residents. In Bergen, the spirit of the Hanseatics lives on, a cherished link to a time when this coastal city played a pivotal role in the tapestry of European trade and commerce.

Trondheim: The Historical Heartland

Trondheim, nestled along the shores of the Trondheimsfjord in central Norway, holds a special place in the country's history and culture. This charming city, with its rich tapestry of historical landmarks and traditions, is often referred to as the historical heartland of Norway.

The origins of Trondheim can be traced back over a thousand years, to the Viking Age when it was known as Nidaros. It was established as a trading post and quickly grew in significance, becoming the seat of royal power in the 11th century. Trondheim's historical importance is closely tied to the establishment of the Nidaros Cathedral, which served as the coronation site for Norwegian monarchs for centuries.

The Nidaros Cathedral, an architectural masterpiece, stands as a symbol of Trondheim's historical significance. Construction of the cathedral began in 1070 and continued for several centuries. Its Romanesque and Gothic elements, intricate sculptures, and stunning stained glass windows make it a testament to the artistry and craftsmanship of the time. Today, it remains one of the most important pilgrimage sites in Northern Europe.

The city's historical charm extends beyond the cathedral. Trondheim's old town, Bakklandet, is a picturesque neighborhood characterized by colorful wooden houses, cobblestone streets, and quaint cafes. Strolling through Bakklandet feels like stepping back in time, offering a glimpse of Trondheim's historical past.

Trondheim has long been a center of education and culture. The city is home to the Norwegian University of Science and Technology (NTNU), one of Norway's leading institutions, with a rich history dating back to 1760. The university's presence has contributed to Trondheim's vibrant intellectual and creative atmosphere.

The city's cultural scene is also enriched by its museums and galleries. The Archbishop's Palace Museum, located near the Nidaros Cathedral, showcases the history of the archbishops who played a pivotal role in Norway's medieval religious and political life. The Rockheim Museum celebrates Norway's music history, with a focus on rock and pop music.

Trondheim's location on the Trondheimsfjord has played a vital role in its development. The fjord, with its strategic position for trade and transportation, has been a lifeline for the city throughout its history. Today, it offers opportunities for recreation and leisure, with boat tours, fishing, and scenic walks along its shores.

One of Trondheim's beloved traditions is the Gamle Bybro, or Old Town Bridge, a picturesque pedestrian bridge adorned with colorful locks left by lovers. Crossing the bridge leads to the idyllic neighborhood of Bakklandet and offers splendid views of the Nidaros Cathedral.

The city's cultural calendar is dotted with events and festivals that celebrate its history and traditions. The St. Olav Festival, named after Norway's patron saint, St. Olav, is a week-long event that combines religious ceremonies, cultural performances, and historical reenactments. It's a time when the city comes alive with a sense of heritage and community.

Trondheim's historical significance is not limited to its past; it continues to shape the city's identity today. Its vibrant blend of history, culture, and natural beauty makes it a captivating destination for travelers and a cherished home for its residents. In Trondheim, the historical heartland of Norway, the past lives on, entwined with the present, creating a living tapestry of traditions and stories that continue to inspire and enchant.

Tromsø: Gateway to the Arctic

Tromsø, perched on the northern tip of Norway's mainland, is a city of unparalleled Arctic beauty and significance. As the largest urban center in the Arctic region, Tromsø serves as a gateway to the icy wilderness of the far north and offers a unique blend of natural wonders, scientific exploration, and cultural richness.

The city's strategic location within the Arctic Circle makes it a natural starting point for Arctic expeditions and research ventures. Tromsø's history as a hub for Arctic exploration can be traced back to the late 19th century when explorers like Roald Amundsen used the city as a base for their polar journeys.

Tromsø's importance as a center for Arctic research continues to this day. The city is home to several research institutions and facilities dedicated to the study of Arctic climate, ecosystems, and geology. The University of Tromsø, known for its polar research programs, plays a central role in advancing our understanding of the Arctic environment.

One of Tromsø's most iconic landmarks is the Arctic Cathedral, a striking piece of modern architecture that resembles an iceberg or a grand cathedral bathed in the ethereal light of the midnight sun. The cathedral's design and interior create a serene space for contemplation and reflection.

Tromsø is renowned as one of the best places on Earth to witness the Northern Lights, also known as the Aurora

Borealis. Its location within the Aurora Oval, a region where the Northern Lights are frequently visible, draws visitors from around the world who yearn to witness this celestial spectacle. The winter months, with their long, dark nights, provide optimal conditions for Aurora hunting.

The city's commitment to preserving its natural surroundings is evident in its network of parks and green spaces. Tromsø's Arctic-Alpine Botanic Garden showcases the unique flora of the region, while the Tromsø Wilderness Centre offers opportunities for wildlife observation and nature experiences.

Tromsø's cultural scene is a testament to its Arctic identity. The Tromsø International Film Festival (TIFF) is a notable event that celebrates Arctic and international cinema. The city's museums, such as the Polaria Arctic Aquarium and the Polar Museum, provide insights into the history and culture of the Arctic peoples.

Tromsø's Arctic cuisine reflects the region's unique flavors and traditions. Seafood, particularly Arctic cod and king crab, is a culinary highlight, while traditional dishes like "reindeer stew" and "mølje" (a fish dish) showcase the tastes of the north. Visitors can savor these delights at local restaurants and eateries.

Tromsø's position on the edge of the Arctic Ocean allows for numerous outdoor adventures. Activities like dog sledding, snowmobiling, and ice fishing are popular winter pursuits, while hiking and kayaking offer unique summer experiences amidst the Arctic landscapes.

The city's Arctic character is not limited to the realm of science and exploration; it's ingrained in the culture, lifestyle, and spirit of its residents. Tromsø's people embrace the Arctic's challenges and beauty, fostering a sense of resilience and wonder that defines life in this Arctic gateway.

In Tromsø, the city that proudly bears the title of "Gateway to the Arctic," the Arctic's majesty and mystery are within reach. It's a place where science and nature converge, where the Northern Lights dance across the night sky, and where culture and tradition thrive in one of the world's most captivating and remote settings. Tromsø is a testament to the enduring allure of the Arctic, a land of endless wonder and discovery.

Stavanger: Oil Capital and Cultural Hub

Stavanger, situated on the southwestern coast of Norway, is a city of intriguing dualities. It wears multiple hats with grace, serving as the oil capital of Norway while also embracing a rich cultural heritage. This dynamic city has emerged as a global player in the energy industry while preserving its historical charm and artistic vibrancy.

The journey of Stavanger's transformation into the oil capital of Norway began in the late 1960s when significant offshore oil reserves were discovered in the North Sea. These discoveries catapulted Norway into the ranks of the world's leading oil and gas producers. Stavanger, strategically located near these offshore oil fields, became the epicenter of Norway's oil industry.

Today, the city is home to numerous international oil companies, including Equinor (formerly Statoil), which plays a pivotal role in the global energy sector. The bustling port of Stavanger serves as a hub for offshore operations, maintenance, and logistics, making it a critical component of Norway's petroleum industry.

Stavanger's Oil & Gas Museum, known locally as the Norsk Oljemuseum, offers an engaging journey through the history of Norway's oil and gas exploration. Visitors can explore interactive exhibits, learn about offshore drilling technology, and gain insights into the challenges and triumphs of the industry.

While Stavanger's economic significance is deeply tied to the oil industry, the city has also embraced its cultural heritage with open arms. The Stavanger Cathedral, dating back to the 12th century, is a symbol of the city's historical importance and serves as a magnificent example of medieval architecture.

Stavanger's old town, Gamle Stavanger, is a charming neighborhood characterized by well-preserved white wooden houses that date back to the 18th and 19th centuries. These quaint streets offer a glimpse into the city's past and provide a serene atmosphere for exploration.

Cultural enthusiasts will find plenty to delight in Stavanger. The Stavanger Symphony Orchestra, one of Norway's leading orchestras, performs in the stunning Stavanger Concert Hall. The city's diverse music scene also includes jazz festivals, rock concerts, and folk music gatherings.

Stavanger's appreciation for the arts extends to its museums and galleries. The Stavanger Art Museum houses an impressive collection of Norwegian and international art, including works by celebrated artists like Edvard Munch. The Norwegian Petroleum Museum offers an in-depth look at the history, technology, and environmental impact of the oil industry.

Foodies will find Stavanger's culinary scene to be a delightful fusion of traditional Norwegian flavors and international influences. Seafood, including salmon, cod, and prawns, features prominently on menus, and visitors can savor these dishes in the city's restaurants and seafood markets.

Stavanger's proximity to the dramatic landscapes of the Lysefjord and Preikestolen (Pulpit Rock) adds an element of natural wonder to the city's allure. Hiking, rock climbing, and boat tours provide opportunities to explore these breathtaking surroundings.

In recent years, Stavanger has also emerged as a center for innovation and sustainability, with a focus on renewable energy, green technologies, and eco-friendly practices. This forward-looking approach aligns with Norway's commitment to environmental responsibility.

Stavanger's ability to balance its role as an oil capital with its vibrant cultural and historical identity is a testament to its resilience and adaptability. It's a city where innovation and tradition coexist, where the legacy of the past informs the promise of the future. In Stavanger, the oil capital and cultural hub, visitors and residents alike can witness the harmonious convergence of industry, culture, and natural beauty in a city that continues to evolve while honoring its roots.

Kristiansand: Coastal Gem of the South

Nestled on the southern coast of Norway, Kristiansand is a coastal gem that captures the essence of Norwegian maritime beauty. With its picturesque waterfront, cultural attractions, and vibrant outdoor scene, this city exudes an irresistible charm that beckons visitors to explore its coastal treasures.

Founded in 1641 by King Christian IV of Denmark-Norway, Kristiansand bears the name of its royal patron. Its strategic location along the Skagerrak strait, which connects the North Sea to the Baltic Sea, has made it a vital center for trade and maritime activities throughout its history.

The city's harbor, known as the Port of Kristiansand, remains a bustling hub for maritime commerce. It accommodates a variety of vessels, from fishing boats to cruise ships, and serves as a gateway to Norway for seafarers and travelers alike.

Kristiansand's coastline is adorned with pristine beaches, making it a popular destination for sun-seekers during the summer months. The city's main beach, Bystranda, offers a relaxing seaside escape, complete with sandy shores, crystal-clear waters, and a picturesque boardwalk. It's a place where locals and tourists gather to soak up the sun and enjoy the refreshing sea breeze.

The city's commitment to preserving its natural beauty is evident in its numerous parks and green spaces. Ravnedalen Park, with its lush flora and tranquil atmosphere, provides a serene escape from the urban hustle and bustle. Baneheia, a nearby forested area with picturesque lakes, offers opportunities for hiking, picnicking, and outdoor adventures.

Kristiansand is also known for its family-friendly attractions. Dyreparken, the city's zoo and amusement park, is a favorite among children and adults alike. It features a wide range of animals, thrilling rides, and interactive exhibits that celebrate Norway's wildlife and culture.

The city's historical heritage can be explored at Kristiansand's open-air museum, Setesdalsbanen Railway, and Kristiansand Museum. These sites offer a glimpse into Norway's past, with well-preserved buildings, artifacts, and exhibits that tell the story of the region's history and traditions.

Kristiansand's cultural scene thrives with theaters, galleries, and festivals. Kilden Performing Arts Center, a modern architectural marvel, hosts a variety of cultural performances, from ballet and opera to concerts and theater productions. The city's cultural calendar is dotted with events, including the Kristiansand International Children's Film Festival and the Punkt Festival, which celebrates experimental music.

Seafood is a culinary highlight in Kristiansand, with fresh catches from the nearby waters making their way to local restaurants and seafood markets. Traditional Norwegian dishes, such as "grilled mackerel" and "rakfisk" (fermented fish), are enjoyed alongside international cuisine in the city's dining establishments.

Kristiansand's maritime history is celebrated at the Kristiansand Cannon Museum, which showcases coastal defenses and military installations from World War II. Visitors can explore bunkers and artillery positions that once played a crucial role in protecting Norway's coast.

The city's dedication to sustainability and eco-friendly practices aligns with Norway's broader commitment to environmental responsibility. Kristiansand's initiatives include renewable energy projects and efforts to reduce greenhouse gas emissions.

In Kristiansand, the coastal gem of the south, visitors encounter a city that harmoniously blends natural beauty, cultural richness, and maritime heritage. It's a place where the shimmering sea meets the lush greenery of parks, where history comes to life, and where the arts thrive. Kristiansand beckons travelers to embrace its coastal allure, inviting them to savor its maritime traditions, explore its cultural treasures, and revel in the beauty of Norway's southern shores.

Molde: The City of Roses

Nestled along the scenic coastline of the Romsdal Peninsula in Norway, Molde is a city that embodies natural beauty, cultural richness, and a unique floral heritage. Known as the "City of Roses," Molde's charm is deeply intertwined with its stunning landscapes, vibrant cultural scene, and the delightful fragrance of its blooming gardens.

The history of Molde dates back to the Viking Age, but it wasn't until the 18th century that it began to flourish as a trading and fishing town. Its strategic location, nestled between the fjords and the sea, made it a hub for maritime activities and trade. However, it was in the 19th century that Molde earned its reputation as the "City of Roses."

The story goes that during the early 19th century, a local bishop, Johan Ernst Gunnerus, introduced roses to Molde. Their cultivation quickly caught on, and the city's residents embraced the idea of transforming Molde into a haven for these beautiful blooms. The favorable climate, with mild winters and long daylight hours during the summer, proved ideal for nurturing a wide variety of roses.

Today, Molde's rose gardens are a testament to this legacy. The Molde International Jazz Festival, often referred to as the Moldejazz, draws jazz enthusiasts and musicians from around the world to the city's lush gardens, where open-air concerts are held amidst the fragrant blossoms. It's a unique fusion of music and nature that has become a hallmark of Molde's cultural identity.

Molde's devotion to the arts extends beyond jazz. The city boasts several cultural institutions, including the Molde International Literature Festival, which celebrates Norwegian and international literature. The Molde International Choir Festival showcases choral music from diverse traditions and cultures, further enriching the city's artistic landscape.

The Molde International Film Festival, known as the Molde International Short Film Festival (MISFF), provides a platform for filmmakers to showcase their short films to a global audience. This annual event reflects Molde's commitment to the cinematic arts and storytelling.

Molde's embrace of its natural surroundings is evident in its outdoor activities. The city is surrounded by stunning fjords and mountains, offering opportunities for hiking, skiing, and water sports. The panoramic view from the Varden viewpoint, accessible by a short hike or a scenic drive, provides a breathtaking vista of the Molde archipelago and the surrounding mountains.

The city's maritime heritage is celebrated at the Molde International Maritime Festival, which showcases traditional boat races, coastal culture, and the importance of the sea to the region's identity. Visitors can explore the Molde International Boat Collection, which houses a remarkable collection of historic boats and artifacts.

Molde's culinary scene is characterized by fresh seafood, including locally caught fish and shellfish. Traditional Norwegian dishes, such as "rakfisk" (fermented fish) and "lutefisk" (dried fish treated with lye), are savored alongside modern international cuisine in the city's restaurants.

Molde's commitment to sustainability and environmental responsibility aligns with Norway's broader efforts to protect its natural surroundings. The city is engaged in green initiatives and renewable energy projects, contributing to Norway's reputation as a leader in eco-friendly practices.

In Molde, the City of Roses, the scent of blooming flowers mingles with the rhythms of jazz, the pages of literature, and the beauty of the outdoors. It's a city that invites travelers to immerse themselves in its cultural tapestry, explore its natural wonders, and embrace the legacy of roses that has left an indelible mark on its identity. Molde, with its unique blend of floral splendor and artistic vibrancy, remains a cherished jewel on Norway's coastal landscape.

Ålesund: Art Nouveau Beauty

Ålesund, a picturesque coastal town on the west coast of Norway, is a true masterpiece of Art Nouveau architecture and natural beauty. Nestled amid the stunning fjords and rugged mountains of the Møre og Romsdal region, this charming town stands as a living testament to the resilience of its people and the transformative power of architectural innovation.

The story of Ålesund's architectural rebirth can be traced back to a devastating fire that swept through the town in January 1904. Nearly the entire town was reduced to ashes, leaving its residents with the daunting task of rebuilding their beloved Ålesund. What followed was nothing short of remarkable.

The rebuilding efforts were led by young Norwegian architects who were inspired by the Art Nouveau movement, characterized by its flowing lines, ornate details, and harmonious design. The result was a town reborn in the embrace of this new architectural style, creating a visual spectacle that stands to this day.

The architectural transformation of Ålesund is particularly evident in its city center. The buildings, adorned with intricate facades, decorative turrets, and whimsical details, reflect the exuberance of the Art Nouveau era. The use of pastel colors adds a touch of vibrancy to the town's skyline, and the harmonious blending of architectural elements creates a unique and enchanting atmosphere.

The Ålesund Town Hall, designed by the renowned architect Sverre Knudsen, is a prime example of the town's Art Nouveau heritage. Its elegant exterior and interior showcase the attention to detail and craftsmanship that define this architectural style.

Ålesund's artistic legacy extends beyond its buildings. The Jugendstilsenteret, or Art Nouveau Center, is a museum dedicated to the Art Nouveau movement and its impact on the town. Visitors can explore exhibitions that delve into the history and artistry of Ålesund's architectural revival.

The natural surroundings of Ålesund are equally captivating. The town is situated amidst the fjords and mountains of the Sunnmøre region, offering breathtaking vistas and outdoor adventures. Hiking, fishing, and boat trips provide opportunities to explore the scenic landscapes and tranquil waters that define this part of Norway.

The coastal location of Ålesund has also influenced its culinary scene. Seafood, including cod, salmon, and prawns, takes center stage on menus, showcasing the freshness of locally sourced ingredients. Traditional Norwegian dishes like "fiskekaker" (fish cakes) and "klippfisk" (dried and salted cod) are celebrated alongside international flavors.

Ålesund's commitment to sustainability and eco-friendly practices aligns with Norway's broader efforts to protect its natural environment. The town is engaged in green initiatives, renewable energy projects, and environmental conservation, reflecting its dedication to preserving the natural beauty that surrounds it.

In Ålesund, the Art Nouveau Beauty, the fusion of architectural splendor and natural grandeur creates an unforgettable experience for visitors. It's a town where history and artistry intersect, where vibrant colors and intricate designs adorn every corner, and where the resilience of a community gave birth to a unique and enduring legacy. Ålesund, with its architectural charm and coastal allure, stands as a testament to the enduring spirit of creativity and renewal.

Narvik: A Railway Adventure

Narvik, a small coastal town nestled in the northern reaches of Norway, is a place that beckons travelers with its unique blend of natural beauty, historical significance, and a railway adventure that is nothing short of spectacular. Situated within the Arctic Circle, Narvik's dramatic landscapes and pivotal role in World War II history make it a destination unlike any other.

The story of Narvik's railway adventure begins with the construction of the Ofotbanen railway, also known as the Ofoten Line. This remarkable railway was completed in 1902 and quickly became a lifeline for transporting iron ore from the mines in Kiruna, Sweden, to the ice-free port of Narvik, where it could be shipped to international markets. The Ofoten Line, with its breathtaking journey through rugged mountains and along fjords, is renowned for its stunning vistas and engineering marvels.

One of the highlights of the Ofoten Line is the steep ascent from sea level to the mining town of Riksgränsen, which lies at an elevation of 912 meters (2,992 feet). This incline, known as the Rombak Rise, is a testament to the engineering prowess of the time and provides passengers with awe-inspiring views of the surrounding landscapes.

The Ofoten Line continues to be an important transportation route, connecting Narvik with Kiruna and providing a vital link for the iron ore industry. Today, the railway offers passengers a unique opportunity to experience the Arctic wilderness in all its splendor. Traveling through the changing landscapes, from coastal vistas to snow-covered mountains, is a journey of pure enchantment.

Narvik's strategic location on the shores of the Ofotfjorden made it a significant naval port during World War II. The town played a pivotal role in the Norwegian Campaign of 1940, with British and Norwegian forces attempting to halt the German advance into Norway. The Battles of Narvik saw intense fighting in the fjords, and the town's history is marked by the bravery of those who defended it.

The Narvik War Museum, located in the town center, pays tribute to the wartime history of Narvik and the surrounding region. Visitors can explore exhibitions that shed light on the events of World War II and the sacrifices made by both military personnel and civilians.

Narvik's natural surroundings are a playground for outdoor enthusiasts. The nearby Narvikfjellet mountain offers skiing and snowboarding in the winter and hiking trails with panoramic views in the summer. The surrounding fjords and coastal areas provide opportunities for fishing, kayaking, and wildlife observation, with the chance to spot reindeer and seabirds.

The town's commitment to sustainability and environmental responsibility aligns with Norway's broader efforts to protect its natural environment. Narvik is actively involved in renewable energy projects and environmental conservation initiatives, ensuring that the pristine Arctic landscapes that surround it are preserved for future generations.

In Narvik, the Railway Adventure, the Ofoten Line offers not just a mode of transportation but a journey through time and nature's grandeur. It's a place where history and wilderness intersect, where the echoes of World War II battles still resonate, and where the rugged beauty of the Arctic captivates the imagination. Narvik stands as a testament to the enduring spirit of exploration and the allure of a railway adventure that traverses some of the most breathtaking landscapes in Norway.

Tromsø: The Arctic City

Tromsø, often referred to as the "Gateway to the Arctic," is a city that sits on the cusp of the Arctic Circle, where snow-capped mountains meet the icy waters of the Norwegian Sea. It's a place where the extremes of the Arctic climate and the warmth of its vibrant culture come together in a harmonious blend that captivates all who venture northward.

This northernmost city in Norway has a rich history that dates back centuries. Established as a trading post in 1252, Tromsø's strategic location made it a hub for Arctic exploration and trade. The city served as a launching point for numerous polar expeditions, including those led by Roald Amundsen, who set out on his quest to conquer the North Pole from Tromsø.

Tromsø's location, well above the Arctic Circle, provides it with unique natural phenomena. During the winter months, the city is plunged into polar darkness, only to be illuminated by the enchanting glow of the Northern Lights, or Aurora Borealis. The ethereal dance of colorful lights in the night sky is a sight that draws visitors from around the world, and Tromsø is one of the prime viewing spots for this celestial spectacle.

The city's Arctic climate, characterized by cold winters and mild summers, makes it a haven for winter sports enthusiasts. Skiing, snowboarding, and dog sledding are popular activities in the surrounding snowy landscapes, while the longer daylight hours of summer offer opportunities for hiking, kayaking, and exploring the rugged wilderness.

Tromsø's commitment to scientific research is evident in its numerous research institutions and the presence of the University of Tromsø, the world's northernmost university. The city has played a crucial role in Arctic research, with scientists studying everything from climate change to marine biology in the Arctic Ocean.

Culturally, Tromsø is a lively and cosmopolitan city. Its thriving arts scene includes theaters, galleries, and music festivals that cater to a diverse range of tastes. The Tromsø International Film Festival (TIFF) is a notable event that celebrates international cinema in the heart of the Arctic.

The Arctic Cathedral, with its distinctive triangular shape and striking stained glass windows, is an iconic landmark that dominates the city's skyline. It serves as both a place of worship and a concert venue, hosting musical performances that resonate within its awe-inspiring interior.

Tromsø's culinary scene reflects its Arctic heritage, with a focus on locally sourced ingredients. Fresh seafood, including cod, salmon, and king crab, is a highlight, as are traditional Norwegian dishes like "lutefisk" (dried fish treated with lye) and "rakfisk" (fermented fish). The city's restaurants offer a delectable fusion of northern flavors and international cuisines.

The presence of indigenous Sámi culture is also significant in Tromsø, with opportunities to learn about and engage with Sámi traditions and heritage. The city's Sámi Week celebrates the indigenous culture of the region through exhibitions, performances, and workshops.

Tromsø's dedication to sustainability and environmental responsibility aligns with Norway's broader commitment to protecting its Arctic environments. The city actively participates in renewable energy projects and conservation efforts to preserve the pristine natural beauty of the Arctic landscapes that surround it.

Tromsø, the Arctic City, stands as a testament to the human spirit's capacity to thrive in the most extreme of environments. It's a place where science and adventure converge, where the celestial wonders of the Northern Lights illuminate the polar night, and where culture and nature coexist in a breathtaking Arctic tableau. Tromsø, with its Arctic allure and warm embrace, is a city that leaves an indelible mark on the souls of those who venture into its frozen embrace.

Sami Culture Today: Preserving Traditions

The Sami people, one of Europe's indigenous groups, have a rich and diverse cultural heritage that spans the northern reaches of Norway, Sweden, Finland, and parts of Russia. Today, Sami culture continues to thrive, adapting to the modern world while steadfastly preserving its ancient traditions and way of life.

One of the defining features of Sami culture is its deep connection to the Arctic environment. Traditionally, the Sami people have been semi-nomadic, relying on reindeer herding, fishing, and hunting for sustenance. Reindeer herding, in particular, holds a central place in Sami culture, providing not only food and clothing but also a strong cultural identity.

Modern Sami reindeer herders continue to practice their ancestral traditions, guiding their herds across vast Arctic landscapes, even as they face the challenges of climate change and land encroachment. The reindeer, known as "buorit" in the Sami language, remain a symbol of resilience and adaptation.

The Sami language, which comprises several distinct dialects, is a cornerstone of cultural preservation. Efforts to revitalize and maintain the Sami language have been ongoing, with schools, language programs, and cultural institutions playing a vital role in passing it down to younger generations. Sami people take great pride in their linguistic heritage and its role in preserving their unique identity.

In the modern era, the Sami people have embraced a range of professions and occupations, including politics, education, arts, and entrepreneurship. Sami parliamentarians have been elected to represent their people in national governments, advocating for Sami rights and cultural preservation. Organizations such as the Sami Council work on an international level to address issues facing Sami communities across borders.

Sami arts and crafts also play a crucial role in cultural preservation. Traditional Sami clothing, known as "gákti," is characterized by intricate designs and patterns that often reflect the wearer's family or community. Additionally, handcrafted items like jewelry, drums, and knives showcase the exquisite craftsmanship of Sami artisans and serve as important cultural artifacts.

The annual Sami National Day, celebrated on February 6th, provides an opportunity for Sami communities to come together and showcase their cultural heritage. Festivals, traditional singing (joik), and the display of traditional clothing are central to these celebrations, fostering a sense of unity and pride among Sami people.

The relationship between the Sami people and the lands they inhabit is a vital aspect of their cultural identity. Sami communities engage in sustainable practices, respecting the environment and preserving their ancestral territories. They are active participants in discussions about environmental conservation and the impact of resource extraction on their lands.

While Sami culture has evolved and adapted to modern life, its essence remains deeply rooted in traditions that have sustained the Sami people for generations. The resilience, determination, and cultural pride of the Sami continue to shine brightly, ensuring that their unique heritage will be carried forward into the future.

In conclusion, Sami Culture Today: Preserving Traditions, reflects the ongoing commitment of the Sami people to maintain their cultural heritage while embracing the challenges and opportunities of the modern world. Their dedication to language, reindeer herding, crafts, and environmental stewardship ensures that the vibrant tapestry of Sami culture endures and thrives in the 21st century.

Norwegian Folk Music and Dance

Norwegian folk music and dance are like windows into the soul of a nation, revealing a rich tapestry of traditions, melodies, and rhythms that have echoed through the country's history for centuries. These cultural expressions are deeply rooted in the Norwegian landscape and the lives of its people, serving as a testament to the enduring spirit of the nation.

Folk music in Norway encompasses a diverse array of styles and regional variations, reflecting the country's vast geographical and cultural diversity. The most iconic of these musical traditions is the "Hardanger fiddle" or "Hardingfele." This unique and beautifully adorned violin-like instrument, characterized by sympathetic strings beneath the fingerboard, produces a hauntingly beautiful sound that is instantly recognizable as Norwegian.

Hardanger fiddle music is often associated with rural and mountainous regions, where it has been played at weddings, celebrations, and gatherings for generations. The tunes are imbued with the natural world, evoking images of towering peaks, cascading waterfalls, and the pristine beauty of Norway's landscapes.

Another prominent form of Norwegian folk music is the "slåtter," or folk dance tunes. These tunes are typically performed on various traditional instruments, including the Hardanger fiddle, accordion, and harmonium. Slåtter are an integral part of Norwegian folk dance, and they accompany a wide range of traditional dance styles, each with its own unique steps and patterns. One of the most beloved

Norwegian folk dances is the "springar." Springar dances are characterized by intricate footwork, often involving hopping and leaping, and they vary from region to region. The exuberance and energy of springar dances are infectious, drawing participants and spectators alike into the lively rhythms of Norwegian folk music.

Another popular dance style is the "pols," which is a faster and more joyful dance, often performed at weddings and festive occasions. The pols features couples whirling and spinning in sync with the music, creating a sense of merriment and camaraderie.

The Sami people, Norway's indigenous inhabitants, have their own distinct musical traditions that reflect their nomadic lifestyle and connection to the Arctic environment. The "joik," a unique form of Sami singing, is a spiritual and deeply emotional expression of their culture. Joiking captures the essence of people, animals, and landscapes in its melodies, making it a cherished aspect of Sami heritage.

Norwegian folk music and dance continue to be celebrated and embraced by both young and old, with numerous festivals, workshops, and cultural events dedicated to preserving and promoting these traditions. The Hønefoss Folk Music Festival and the Telemark Festival are just two examples of gatherings that bring together musicians, dancers, and enthusiasts from across Norway and beyond.

In recent years, contemporary artists and musicians have infused new life into Norwegian folk music, blending traditional elements with modern influences. This fusion has brought this cultural treasure into the 21st century, ensuring its relevance and vibrancy for future generations.

Norwegian Literature: From the Sagas to Modern Novels

The literary tradition of Norway is a tapestry woven with threads of history, culture, and the natural world, resulting in a rich and diverse body of work that spans from the ancient sagas to contemporary novels. Norwegian literature has long been a reflection of the nation's identity, its relationship with nature, and its exploration of the human condition.

The roots of Norwegian literature delve deep into the past, with the Viking Age sagas serving as some of the earliest recorded narratives. These sagas, including the famous "Edda" and "Heimskringla," chronicle the adventures, myths, and legends of the Norse people. The sagas are a testament to the oral storytelling tradition of the Vikings and have left an indelible mark on world literature.

In the Middle Ages, Norway's literature continued to evolve, with the sagas giving way to the development of written texts. One of the most significant works of this period is the "Kongespeilet" or "The King's Mirror," a 13th-century instructional text that offers insights into Norwegian society, culture, and ethics. It provides a window into the intellectual and moral concerns of the time.

The Reformation in the 16th century brought about a shift in literary focus, with religious texts and hymns becoming prominent. The translation of the Bible into Norwegian by

Hans Nielsen Hauge played a pivotal role in shaping the language and literature of Norway.

The 19th century marked a significant turning point in Norwegian literature, often referred to as the "Golden Age." This era saw the emergence of literary giants like Henrik Ibsen, Bjørnstjerne Bjørnson, and Alexander Kielland. Henrik Ibsen, in particular, is celebrated as one of the most influential playwrights in world literature, known for groundbreaking works like "A Doll's House" and "Peer Gynt." His plays explored social issues and the complexities of human relationships, sparking conversations and debates far beyond Norway's borders.

Bjørnstjerne Bjørnson, a contemporary of Ibsen, was a prolific writer and poet who won the Nobel Prize in Literature in 1903. His works often focused on themes of national identity and social justice, contributing to the broader cultural and political discussions of his time.

Norwegian literature continued to flourish in the 20th and 21st centuries, with authors like Knut Hamsun, Sigrid Undset, and more recently, Karl Ove Knausgård, gaining international acclaim. Hamsun's novel "Hunger" is a masterpiece of modernist literature, while Sigrid Undset's historical novels, including "Kristin Lavransdatter," earned her the Nobel Prize in Literature in 1928.

Karl Ove Knausgård's six-volume autobiographical novel series, "My Struggle" (Min Kamp), has garnered widespread attention for its raw and unflinching exploration of personal experiences. The series has been both celebrated and controversial, sparking discussions about the boundaries of memoir and fiction.

Contemporary Norwegian literature continues to thrive, with authors like Jo Nesbø, Per Petterson, and Maja Lunde gaining recognition for their contributions to various genres, including crime fiction, literary fiction, and environmental themes.

In conclusion, Norwegian literature is a dynamic and ever-evolving reflection of the nation's history, culture, and identity. From the sagas of old to the modern novels of today, it serves as a literary journey through time, offering profound insights into the human experience and the enduring spirit of Norway.

Contemporary Norwegian Art and Artists

The world of contemporary Norwegian art is a vibrant and diverse landscape, where artists explore a wide range of themes, techniques, and mediums. It's a realm where tradition meets innovation, and where the country's stunning natural landscapes continue to inspire creativity. Let's delve into the world of contemporary Norwegian art and discover some of the talented artists who have left their mark on the global art scene.

One prominent figure in contemporary Norwegian art is Edvard Munch, best known for his iconic painting "The Scream." While Munch's work is often associated with the late 19th and early 20th centuries, his influence on modern and contemporary art is undeniable. His exploration of the human psyche and emotions laid the groundwork for subsequent generations of Norwegian artists to delve into the depths of their own creativity.

In the mid-20th century, Norwegian art saw the emergence of abstract expressionism and modernism. Artists like Ludvig Eikaas and Jakob Weidemann contributed to these movements, experimenting with color, form, and abstraction in their works. Their bold and innovative approaches to painting challenged traditional norms and expanded the horizons of Norwegian art.

The late 20th century brought a wave of contemporary Norwegian artists who gained international recognition. One such artist is Odd Nerdrum, known for his figurative paintings that often explore themes of existentialism and the human condition. His distinctive style, characterized by thick impasto and dramatic lighting, has earned him a dedicated following worldwide.

Bjarne Melgaard is another contemporary artist who has made waves both in Norway and beyond. His provocative and sometimes controversial works span various mediums, including painting, sculpture, and installation art. Melgaard's exploration of taboo subjects and societal norms challenges viewers to confront uncomfortable truths.

In recent years, the contemporary art scene in Norway has continued to evolve and diversify. Artists like Matias Faldbakken have gained recognition for their conceptual art, while Sverre Bjertnæs has explored themes of identity and culture through his striking figurative paintings. The boundary-pushing works of these artists have garnered attention on the global stage, solidifying Norway's presence in the contemporary art world.

The contemporary Norwegian art scene is not confined to traditional mediums alone. It embraces multimedia and interdisciplinary approaches, with artists like Tori Wraanes and HC Gilje exploring the intersection of technology and art. Their immersive installations and video art challenge viewers to engage with art in new and innovative ways.

Norway's commitment to nurturing artistic talent is evident in institutions like the Oslo National Academy of the Arts, which provides a platform for emerging artists to hone their skills and experiment with their craft. These institutions play a crucial role in fostering the next generation of Norwegian artists who will shape the future of contemporary art.

In conclusion, contemporary Norwegian art is a dynamic and evolving tapestry that reflects the nation's cultural diversity, creative spirit, and engagement with global artistic movements. From the pioneering work of Edvard Munch to the boundary-pushing explorations of today's artists, Norway continues to make its mark on the international art scene, offering a compelling glimpse into the artistic zeitgeist of the country.

Religious Diversity in Norway

Norway, a country known for its breathtaking landscapes, rich cultural heritage, and progressive social policies, is also home to a diverse religious landscape. While historically associated with Christianity, particularly Lutheranism, Norway has witnessed significant changes in its religious demographics over the years, reflecting a broader global trend towards religious diversity and pluralism.

Christianity has deep historical roots in Norway, dating back to the Viking Age when the country converted to Christianity under King Olaf Tryggvason in the 10th century. Lutheranism, in particular, has played a central role in shaping Norwegian religious identity, and the Evangelical Lutheran Church of Norway remains the largest religious denomination in the country. The church is not only a place of worship but also an integral part of Norwegian culture and social life, hosting events, celebrations, and ceremonies.

In recent decades, however, there has been a notable shift in religious affiliation in Norway. The percentage of Norwegians identifying as Christians has declined, while the number of individuals identifying as non-religious or atheists has increased. This trend is in line with broader secularization patterns seen in many Western countries.

Religious diversity in Norway extends beyond Christianity. Islam is one of the fastest-growing religions in the country, with a significant Muslim population, primarily composed of immigrants and their descendants. Mosques and Islamic centers have been established in various Norwegian cities, providing places of worship and community for Muslims. The practice of Islam is protected by law, ensuring freedom of religion for all residents.

Another prominent religious community in Norway is Buddhism. Over the years, Buddhism has gained adherents among both Norwegian-born individuals and immigrants. Buddhist centers and meditation groups are present in several cities, offering spiritual guidance and a sense of community.

Judaism also has a small but historically significant presence in Norway. The Jewish community has faced challenges, particularly during World War II when many Norwegian Jews were persecuted and deported by the Nazi regime. Today, the Jewish community in Norway is small but resilient, with a synagogue in Oslo serving as a focal point for Jewish religious and cultural activities.

Norway has also seen an increase in religious diversity through immigration. As the country has welcomed people from various parts of the world, it has become home to adherents of Hinduism, Sikhism, and other faiths. Temples and gurdwaras (Sikh places of worship) have been established to serve the religious needs of these communities.

Additionally, there is a growing interest in indigenous spiritual practices, particularly among the Sami people of northern Norway. Traditional Sami spirituality, which includes beliefs in nature spirits and shamanistic practices, continues to be a vital part of Sami culture.

Norway's commitment to religious freedom and tolerance is enshrined in its constitution. The country's secular government ensures that individuals have the right to practice their faith or choose not to adhere to any religion. This commitment to religious freedom aligns with Norway's broader values of inclusivity and respect for diversity.

In conclusion, religious diversity in Norway is a reflection of the country's evolving identity and its place in a globalized world. While Christianity, especially Lutheranism, remains deeply ingrained in Norwegian culture, the presence of other religious communities and the rise of non-religious identities highlight the nation's commitment to inclusivity and religious freedom. Norway's religious landscape continues to evolve, reflecting the ever-changing dynamics of society and the world at large.

Christmas in Norway: A Season of Traditions

Christmas in Norway is a time of magic, where centuries-old traditions blend seamlessly with modern festivities. It's a season when families come together to celebrate the warmth of togetherness, the beauty of the winter landscape, and the rich cultural heritage that defines this Scandinavian nation.

The holiday season officially kicks off on December 1st, when many Norwegians begin decorating their homes. One of the most iconic decorations is the Advent calendar, which helps build anticipation as children open a new door or window each day leading up to Christmas Eve.

Christmas trees play a central role in Norwegian celebrations. Families typically gather to decorate the tree on the evening of December 23rd, and it remains the focal point of the home throughout the holiday season. Norwegian Christmas trees are adorned with a mix of traditional and modern ornaments, along with strings of lights and candles.

Candles are a recurring theme in Norwegian Christmas traditions. Many households place electric candles in windows to symbolize the welcoming of Mary and Joseph on their journey to Bethlehem. Additionally, the Christmas Eve candlelight service at churches across Norway is a cherished tradition, where the soft glow of candles creates a serene and magical atmosphere.

Norwegian Christmas Eve, known as "Julekveld," is the most significant day of the holiday season. Families gather for a festive meal that typically includes a variety of dishes, with lamb, pork, or fish often taking center stage. A common dessert is "riskrem," a creamy rice pudding served with raspberry sauce. Hidden within one portion of riskrem is a single almond, and the lucky person who finds it wins a marzipan pig.

After the meal, families exchange gifts, and children eagerly await a visit from Santa Claus or "Julenissen." In Norway, Santa is often depicted as a gnome-like figure who arrives with a sack full of presents. The tradition of giving and receiving gifts on Christmas Eve adds an extra layer of excitement to the holiday.

As the night progresses, many Norwegians attend the aforementioned candlelight church service, where they participate in carol singing and reflect on the meaning of the holiday. Churches are beautifully decorated for the occasion, creating a sense of tranquility and reverence.

December 25th, known as "Første juledag" (First Christmas Day), is another day for gatherings with family and friends. It's common for Norwegians to enjoy a leisurely breakfast and extend the festivities with more food, conversation, and perhaps some outdoor activities if weather permits.

One particularly unique Norwegian Christmas tradition is the "julebukk," where children dress up in costumes and visit neighbors, singing songs and receiving treats. This tradition has its roots in ancient pagan rituals and adds an element of whimsy to the holiday season.

In some parts of Norway, especially in the northern regions, the indigenous Sami people celebrate their own version of Christmas with their unique cultural elements. Reindeer play a significant role in Sami traditions, and their herding and use for transportation are integral to the holiday festivities.

In conclusion, Christmas in Norway is a time when traditions are cherished and celebrated with great enthusiasm. It's a season of warmth, togetherness, and reflection on the enduring cultural heritage that makes Norway's holiday season truly magical. The blending of old and new traditions, along with a deep connection to the natural world, makes Norwegian Christmas a time of joy and wonder for all who embrace it.

Education in Norway: A Model System

Norway's education system stands as a shining example of excellence and equity on the global stage. Rooted in principles of accessibility, inclusivity, and quality, the Norwegian educational model has consistently garnered international recognition. It's a system that not only prioritizes academic achievement but also places a strong emphasis on fostering holistic development, critical thinking, and lifelong learning.

One of the foundational pillars of Norwegian education is its commitment to equal opportunities for all. Education in Norway is free, from primary school through university. This inclusivity ensures that socio-economic status does not act as a barrier to accessing quality education. Regardless of their background, Norwegian students have the same opportunities to pursue their educational aspirations.

The Norwegian education system is divided into several levels, beginning with "Barnehage" (kindergarten), which is optional but highly encouraged for young children. The next phase is "Grunnskole," which covers primary and lower secondary education, spanning from age 6 to 16. Grunnskole focuses on providing a well-rounded education that includes not only core subjects like mathematics and language but also physical education, arts, and ethics.

One unique feature of the Norwegian Grunnskole system is the absence of formal testing and grading until the final year of lower secondary education. Instead, the emphasis is placed on formative assessment, where teachers provide continuous feedback to help students develop their skills and knowledge. This approach fosters a more relaxed and student-centric learning environment, reducing the stress associated with standardized testing.

Upper secondary education in Norway offers students a choice between general academic studies ("Studieforberedende") and vocational programs ("Yrkesfag"). The flexibility of the system allows students to tailor their education to their interests and career goals. For instance, students can choose to pursue specialized vocational training in fields such as healthcare, technology, or the arts.

One hallmark of Norwegian education is its emphasis on student well-being and the promotion of a balanced lifestyle. Physical activity is integrated into the curriculum, and outdoor education is encouraged, capitalizing on Norway's stunning natural landscapes. This focus on student health and outdoor experiences contributes to the country's high quality of life and well-being.

When it comes to higher education, Norway boasts a robust network of universities and colleges. Higher education is also free for both Norwegian and international students, with many programs taught in English to accommodate the diverse student body. The country consistently ranks high in global education rankings, reflecting the quality and rigor of its higher education institutions.

In addition to formal education, Norway places a strong emphasis on lifelong learning and adult education. Opportunities for adults to return to education and acquire new skills are readily available, contributing to a highly educated and adaptable workforce.

The success of the Norwegian education system is further evidenced by the country's high literacy rates, low dropout rates, and the impressive performance of its students in international assessments. Norwegian educators are highly trained and respected professionals, and the country invests significantly in educational research and innovation.

In conclusion, education in Norway is a testament to the country's commitment to equality, inclusivity, and excellence. It's a model system that values both academic achievement and the overall well-being of its students. Through its holistic approach to education, Norway not only prepares students for academic success but also equips them with the skills, knowledge, and values necessary to thrive in a rapidly changing world.

The Norwegian Welfare State: Social Equality

The Norwegian welfare state is a shining example of a society that places a premium on social equality, where citizens enjoy a high standard of living, access to quality healthcare, education, and a safety net that ensures even the most vulnerable are protected. It's a model that other nations often look to emulate, and for good reason.

At the core of the Norwegian welfare state is the principle of universalism. This means that social benefits and services are available to all citizens, regardless of their income, social status, or background. Whether you're a wealthy business owner or an ordinary worker, you have equal access to healthcare, education, and other social services. This commitment to universalism underpins the Norwegian idea of social equality.

One of the key pillars of the Norwegian welfare state is its comprehensive healthcare system. Norway provides its citizens with access to quality healthcare services that are largely funded through taxation. This means that medical treatment is available to everyone, and patients don't have to worry about the financial burden of seeking medical care. It's a system that emphasizes preventive care, early diagnosis, and a patient's right to choose their healthcare provider.

Education is another cornerstone of the Norwegian welfare state. From kindergarten through university, education is not only free but of a high standard. This ensures that every child, regardless of their family's financial situation, has the same educational opportunities. Norwegian students consistently perform well in international assessments, showcasing the effectiveness of the education system.

Work-life balance is highly valued in Norway, with the average workweek being shorter than in many other countries. Employees are entitled to a minimum of five weeks of paid vacation, contributing to a strong emphasis on leisure time, family, and personal well-being. The labor market is also characterized by strong workers' rights and protections.

The Norwegian welfare state also places a significant emphasis on gender equality. Women have equal opportunities in the workforce, and policies such as generous parental leave and subsidized childcare support both mothers and fathers in balancing work and family life. Norway consistently ranks high in global gender equality rankings.

A robust social safety net ensures that those facing temporary or long-term hardships receive the support they need. Unemployment benefits, disability pensions, and other forms of social assistance are designed to provide a safety net for citizens facing economic challenges. The goal is to prevent poverty and ensure that everyone has a basic standard of living.

Norway's welfare state is funded through high taxation, particularly on wealth and income. The country's progressive tax system means that those with higher incomes contribute a larger share of their earnings to support the welfare system. This taxation model helps fund the comprehensive social services that are the hallmark of the Norwegian welfare state.

The Norwegian welfare state is not without its challenges. The aging population and increased immigration have put pressure on the system, prompting discussions about sustainability and potential reforms. Nevertheless, Norway's commitment to social equality and the well-being of its citizens remains steadfast.

In conclusion, the Norwegian welfare state is a testament to the country's dedication to social equality and the well-being of its citizens. It's a model that has successfully combined a strong economy with comprehensive social services, ensuring that everyone has an opportunity to thrive and that no one is left behind. Norway's commitment to universalism, healthcare, education, gender equality, and social safety nets has created a society where social equality is not just a principle but a lived reality.

Norway's Green Initiatives: Sustainability and Conservation

Norway has made substantial strides in recent years in its commitment to sustainability and environmental conservation. Situated amidst breathtaking natural landscapes, Norwegians have recognized the importance of preserving their pristine environment for future generations. From renewable energy to eco-friendly transportation and responsible resource management, Norway's green initiatives are a testament to its dedication to sustainable living.

One of Norway's most significant green achievements is its commitment to renewable energy sources. The country has harnessed its abundant natural resources to become a global leader in renewable energy production. Hydropower, in particular, plays a pivotal role in Norway's energy portfolio. Its extensive network of hydropower plants generates clean electricity, and the surplus is often exported to neighboring countries, reducing their reliance on fossil fuels.

Norway's dedication to electric mobility is another noteworthy green initiative. The country has been at the forefront of promoting electric vehicles (EVs) and has one of the highest per capita rates of EV ownership in the world. Incentives such as tax breaks, toll exemptions, and free parking for electric cars have spurred their adoption. Moreover, Norway's commitment to expanding the charging infrastructure has made EVs a convenient and eco-conscious choice for its citizens.

In the realm of public transportation, Norway has invested heavily in sustainable options. Its cities boast efficient and extensive tram and bus networks, reducing the need for private car ownership. Many urban areas have also implemented bike-sharing programs and pedestrian-friendly infrastructure, encouraging greener modes of transport.

Norwegian cities are designed with sustainability in mind, emphasizing compact urban planning and energy-efficient buildings. Oslo, for instance, has ambitious plans to reduce carbon emissions and become carbon neutral by 2030. Initiatives include retrofitting buildings for energy efficiency, expanding public transportation, and investing in renewable energy sources.

Conservation efforts are integral to Norway's green initiatives. The country's rugged landscapes are home to diverse ecosystems, including its famous fjords, forests, and Arctic regions. Norway has implemented strict regulations on fishing, hunting, and forestry to protect its natural habitats and wildlife. The government also supports research and monitoring programs to better understand and safeguard its fragile Arctic environment.

Norway's commitment to sustainability extends to its responsible management of natural resources. The fishing industry, a vital component of the Norwegian economy, adheres to strict quotas and sustainable practices to ensure the long-term health of marine ecosystems. Additionally, the country has imposed strict environmental regulations on its oil and gas industry to minimize its impact on the environment.

International cooperation is also a cornerstone of Norway's green initiatives. The country actively participates in global climate agreements and contributes to initiatives aimed at combating climate change and protecting biodiversity. Norway's investments in tropical forest conservation and clean energy projects in developing countries further demonstrate its commitment to global sustainability.

In conclusion, Norway's green initiatives exemplify its dedication to a sustainable and environmentally conscious future. From renewable energy production to electric mobility, urban planning, conservation efforts, and responsible resource management, Norway has emerged as a role model in the global quest for a greener, more sustainable world. Its breathtaking natural landscapes serve as a constant reminder of the importance of preserving our planet for generations to come.

The Norwegian Language: Bokmål and Nynorsk

The Norwegian language is a rich and diverse tapestry that reflects the country's complex linguistic history and cultural heritage. Norway, a nation known for its stunning landscapes and vibrant cities, is also home to two official written forms of the language: Bokmål and Nynorsk. These linguistic variations have deep historical roots and continue to shape the Norwegian identity today.

Bokmål, which translates to "book language," is the more widely used and recognized of the two written forms. It is based primarily on the Danish-influenced Norwegian spoken in and around Oslo and other urban areas. Bokmål is often considered the standard Norwegian language and serves as the primary medium of instruction in schools, government, and the media. It is used by a significant majority of Norwegians, especially in urban regions and the southern parts of the country.

Nynorsk, meaning "New Norwegian," is the other official written form and represents a departure from the Danish-influenced language that dominated written Norwegian for centuries. It emerged in the 19th century as part of a broader cultural and nationalistic movement to reclaim Norway's linguistic identity. Nynorsk is primarily based on rural dialects and reflects a desire to preserve and promote the rich tapestry of Norway's regional languages. It is estimated that around 10-15% of Norwegians use Nynorsk as their written language of choice.

The coexistence of Bokmål and Nynorsk as official written forms of Norwegian is enshrined in the country's language policy and constitution. This linguistic duality is a unique feature of Norway and is aimed at preserving linguistic diversity and allowing individuals to express themselves in their preferred written form.

Both Bokmål and Nynorsk have their own standardized grammatical rules, spelling, and vocabulary. They share a common core of words and phrases, but their differences become more pronounced when it comes to vocabulary choices and specific grammatical constructions. For instance, some words and expressions may have different forms in each language.

To accommodate the coexistence of these written forms, Norway's educational system provides instruction in both Bokmål and Nynorsk. Students typically learn to read and write in their local dialect and one of the official written forms, depending on their geographical location. This approach allows students to be bilingual in their written language skills.

The choice of which written form to use is often a matter of personal preference, regional identity, or family tradition. Some Norwegians feel a strong connection to their local dialects and choose Nynorsk as a way to honor and preserve their linguistic heritage. Others may opt for Bokmål for practical reasons, especially if they live in urban areas or work in professions where Bokmål is the dominant written form.

It's worth noting that spoken Norwegian, while influenced by both Bokmål and Nynorsk, is generally more unified and mutually intelligible. The written forms, with their distinct vocabulary and grammar, are where the differences are most apparent.

In conclusion, the Norwegian language, with its two official written forms of Bokmål and Nynorsk, is a reflection of the country's linguistic diversity and cultural heritage. This linguistic duality is embraced as a means of preserving regional dialects and allowing individuals to express themselves in their preferred written form.

Learning Norwegian: Tips for Language Enthusiasts

Embarking on the journey of learning a new language is a rewarding and enriching experience, and when it comes to Norwegian, there's a wealth of linguistic and cultural treasures waiting to be explored. Whether you're a language enthusiast, a traveler, or someone with ties to Norway, here are some valuable tips to help you on your path to mastering the Norwegian language.

1. **Start with the Basics**: Like any language, Norwegian has its fundamentals. Begin by learning the Norwegian alphabet, pronunciation, and basic greetings. Familiarize yourself with common phrases and everyday expressions.
2. **Choose Your Path**: Norwegian has two official written forms, Bokmål and Nynorsk, as discussed earlier. Decide which one you'd like to focus on or whether you'd like to learn both. Your choice may be influenced by personal preference, regional ties, or practical considerations.
3. **Immerse Yourself**: Language immersion is a powerful way to learn. If you have the opportunity, spend time in Norway or engage with native speakers. Conversing with locals can accelerate your language skills and expose you to authentic pronunciation and idioms.
4. **Online Resources**: The internet offers a plethora of resources for language learners. There are numerous language learning apps, websites, and forums dedicated to Norwegian. Duolingo, Memrise, and

Babbel are popular choices. YouTube channels and podcasts can also be valuable for listening practice.

5. **Take Formal Classes**: Consider enrolling in formal language classes if they're available in your area. Many universities and language schools offer Norwegian courses. Structured learning can provide a strong foundation and access to experienced instructors.

6. **Grammar and Vocabulary**: Pay attention to Norwegian grammar and expand your vocabulary systematically. Invest time in understanding verb conjugations, noun genders, and sentence structure. Create flashcards to build your vocabulary.

7. **Reading and Writing**: Reading Norwegian texts and writing in the language are essential for proficiency. Start with simple texts, such as children's books or news articles, and gradually work your way up to more complex literature.

8. **Language Exchange Partners**: Finding a language exchange partner who speaks Norwegian can be immensely beneficial. You can practice speaking and receive feedback, while you can help them with your native language in return.

9. **Cultural Engagement**: Learning a language is not just about words; it's about culture too. Dive into Norwegian culture by watching Norwegian films, TV shows, and listening to Norwegian music. Understanding cultural references enhances your language comprehension.

10. **Persistence and Patience**: Language learning is a marathon, not a sprint. Be patient with yourself and practice regularly. Consistency is key to progress. Set achievable goals and celebrate your milestones along the way.

11. **Visit Norway**: If possible, visit Norway to immerse yourself in the language and culture. Being in a Norwegian-speaking environment can accelerate your learning and deepen your understanding of the language.
12. **Celebrate Norwegian Holidays**: Learning about Norwegian holidays and traditions can be a fun way to connect with the culture and learn new vocabulary related to specific celebrations.
13. **Language Apps**: Mobile apps like Tandem and HelloTalk connect you with native Norwegian speakers for language exchange. These apps allow you to chat and practice with real people.
14. **Online Communities**: Join online forums and communities where learners and native speakers interact. Websites like Reddit have Norwegian-language subreddits where you can ask questions and engage in discussions.
15. **Travel Phrasebook**: Carry a travel phrasebook with you when visiting Norway. It can be a handy reference for common phrases and expressions while you're on the go.

Remember that language learning is a personal journey, and there's no one-size-fits-all approach. Tailor your learning experience to your interests and goals, and enjoy the process of discovering the beauty of the Norwegian language. Whether you aspire to have conversations with locals, delve into Norwegian literature, or simply connect with your heritage, the effort you put into learning Norwegian will be richly rewarded.

Norwegian Holidays and Festivals

In the heart of Scandinavia, Norway is a country steeped in tradition and culture, and its calendar is dotted with vibrant holidays and festivals that reflect the spirit of its people. From ancient celebrations rooted in Norse mythology to modern festivities, Norway offers a rich tapestry of events that showcase its history, heritage, and love for the outdoors.

1. **Norwegian National Day (May 17th)**: May 17th is a day of patriotic pride and merriment for Norwegians. It marks the signing of the Norwegian Constitution in 1814 and the country's independence from Denmark. People don their bunads (traditional costumes), wave the Norwegian flag, and participate in parades, concerts, and festivities.

2. **Midsummer's Eve (June 23rd)**: Known as "Sankthansaften," this celebration takes place on the eve of June 24th, marking the summer solstice. Norwegians light bonfires by the water, sing songs, and enjoy the long, bright summer night. It's a time to embrace nature and the magical ambiance of the season.

3. **St. Olav Festival (July 29th)**: Named after Norway's patron saint, St. Olav, this festival in Trondheim commemorates the saint's death. Pilgrims, musicians, and artists converge on the city for a week of concerts, historical reenactments, and religious ceremonies.

4. **Bergen International Festival (May/June)**: This renowned cultural event in Bergen features a diverse

array of music, theater, dance, and art performances. It draws artists and spectators from around the world and adds a vibrant cultural dimension to Norway's calendar.

5. **Julebord (Christmas Parties)**: In the lead-up to Christmas, Norwegians gather for festive parties known as "julebord." These events are filled with food, drinks, dancing, and merriment. It's a time for coworkers, friends, and families to come together and celebrate.

6. **Norse Mythology Celebrations**: Norway's rich Norse heritage is celebrated through various events and festivals. In places like Lofoten and Avaldsnes, you can find reenactments, storytelling, and festivities dedicated to the gods and legends of Norse mythology.

7. **Northern Lights Festivals**: In the northern regions of Norway, where the magical Northern Lights dance across the sky, you'll find festivals celebrating this celestial phenomenon. These events offer a unique opportunity to witness the Aurora Borealis while enjoying cultural activities and traditional Sami experiences.

8. **Sami National Day (February 6th)**: The Sami people, Norway's indigenous population, have their own national day. This day is dedicated to celebrating Sami culture through events like reindeer races, traditional food, and colorful clothing.

9. **Lillehammer Winter Festival (February)**: As a nation known for its winter sports, Norway hosts numerous winter festivals. Lillehammer's festival features ski races, snow sculptures, and family-friendly activities in the snow-covered landscapes.

10. **Oslo Jazz Festival (August)**: Jazz enthusiasts will find their groove at the Oslo Jazz Festival, which showcases international and Norwegian jazz artists in various venues throughout the city.

11. **Christmas Markets**: As the holiday season approaches, Christmas markets pop up in cities and towns across Norway. These markets are a treasure trove of handmade crafts, seasonal treats, and a festive atmosphere that warms the hearts of locals and visitors alike.

12. **Food Festivals**: Norway's culinary scene is celebrated in food festivals throughout the year. From the Bergen Fish Festival to the Rakfisk Festival, these events allow foodies to indulge in the country's delicious seafood and traditional dishes.

13. **Røros Winter Market (February)**: This historic mining town hosts a winter market where artisans, craftsmen, and traders come together to sell their wares. It's a charming way to experience Norwegian culture and pick up unique souvenirs.

14. **Festspillene i Nord-Norge (Northern Norway Festival)**: This annual festival showcases music, theater, and art from the northern regions of Norway. It's a cultural extravaganza that highlights the unique creativity of the north.

15. **Førde International Folk Music Festival**: Folk music enthusiasts should not miss this festival, which features folk musicians from Norway and around the world. It's a celebration of diverse musical traditions.

These are just a glimpse into the colorful tapestry of holidays and festivals that adorn the Norwegian calendar throughout the year. Each event carries its own unique significance and offers a chance for both locals and visitors to immerse themselves in the rich culture and traditions that make Norway a truly extraordinary country. Whether you're dancing around a bonfire on Midsummer's Eve or savoring traditional dishes at a Christmas market, Norway's holidays and festivals are a vibrant reflection of its history, culture, and community spirit.

Outdoor Adventures in Norway: Hiking, Skiing, and More

Nestled among breathtaking fjords, towering mountains, and pristine forests, Norway is a paradise for outdoor enthusiasts seeking adventure in nature's embrace. Whether you're a hiker, skier, or simply someone who relishes the great outdoors, Norway's landscape offers a diverse range of activities that will leave you awe-inspired and yearning for more.

Hiking in the Norwegian Wilderness

For avid hikers, Norway presents a tapestry of hiking trails that wind through some of Europe's most striking wilderness. The country's "allemannsrett" or "freedom to roam" law allows everyone to explore the countryside, making hiking accessible to all. Here are some remarkable hiking destinations:

- **Trolltunga**: Known as the "Troll's Tongue," this iconic rock formation juts out high above Lake Ringedalsvatnet, offering a panoramic vista that's both thrilling and awe-inspiring. It's a challenging trek but worth every step.
- **Preikestolen (Pulpit Rock)**: A short drive from Stavanger, this flat-topped cliff soars 604 meters above the Lysefjord. The hike to the top rewards you with a breathtaking view of the fjord below.
- **Besseggen Ridge**: Located in Jotunheimen National Park, this challenging hike takes you along a narrow ridge with stunning views of the emerald-green

Gjende Lake on one side and the deep blue Bessvatnet Lake on the other.

- **Hardangervidda**: Norway's largest national park, Hardangervidda, is a vast plateau filled with hiking trails that cross open landscapes, pristine rivers, and offer encounters with wild reindeer.
- **Lofoten Islands**: The dramatic and picturesque landscapes of the Lofoten Islands are a hiker's dream. Explore trails that take you through fishing villages, white sandy beaches, and rugged peaks.

Winter Wonderland: Skiing and Snow Sports

When winter blankets Norway in snow, the country transforms into a playground for snow sports enthusiasts. Whether you're into alpine skiing, cross-country skiing, snowboarding, or even dog sledding, Norway's winter sports offerings are world-class:

- **Trysil**: Norway's largest ski resort, Trysil offers a variety of slopes and trails suitable for skiers of all levels. It's also known for its modern amenities and family-friendly atmosphere.
- **Hemsedal**: This ski resort is renowned for its extensive terrain, making it a favorite among advanced skiers and snowboarders. It boasts a vibrant après-ski scene too.
- **Cross-Country Skiing**: Norway is the birthplace of cross-country skiing, and you'll find countless well-groomed trails, including the famous Birkebeinerrennet route from Rena to Lillehammer.
- **Svalbard**: For a truly unique winter adventure, head to Svalbard, where you can explore the Arctic wilderness, go snowmobiling, and even witness the mesmerizing Northern Lights.

Fishing and Water Adventures

Norway's coastline is a haven for fishing enthusiasts. From deep-sea fishing for cod and halibut to fly fishing for salmon in the country's rivers, there's a fishing experience for everyone.

- **Whale Watching**: Norway's coastal waters are home to various whale species. Embark on a whale-watching excursion to catch a glimpse of these magnificent creatures.
- **Kayaking and Canoeing**: The country's numerous lakes, fjords, and rivers offer fantastic opportunities for paddling adventures. Explore secluded coves or navigate your way through dramatic fjords.
- **Climbing and Mountaineering**: Norway's mountains provide a challenging playground for climbers and mountaineers. Whether you're a beginner or an experienced alpinist, there are routes to suit your skill level.

Camping and Wildlife Encounters

For those who relish the simplicity of camping and the thrill of wildlife encounters, Norway delivers:

- **Wild Camping**: Thanks to allemannsrett, you can set up camp almost anywhere in the countryside. Wake up to the sounds of nature and the beauty of untouched landscapes.
- **Wildlife Safaris**: Join a wildlife safari to spot moose, reindeer, lynx, and even the elusive Arctic polar bear in its natural habitat.

- **Bird Watching**: Norway is a bird-watcher's paradise, with numerous bird species inhabiting its varied landscapes.

Rock Climbing and Via Ferrata

Rock climbers and adventure seekers can conquer towering cliffs and mountain faces. Places like Romsdalen, Kjerag, and the Setesdal Valley offer challenging climbs and via ferrata routes.

Biking and Cycling

Norway's cycling routes cater to both road cyclists and mountain bikers. The country's rugged terrain and scenic byways make it an ideal destination for bike enthusiasts.

Norse Folklore and Superstitions

Throughout the rich tapestry of Norse culture and history, folklore and superstitions have played a significant role in shaping the beliefs and traditions of the people of Scandinavia. These stories and beliefs, passed down through generations, offer a glimpse into the mystical world of the Norse and their deep connection to the natural forces that surrounded them.

The World of Norse Mythology

At the heart of Norse folklore lies a pantheon of gods and goddesses, each with their own unique powers and personalities. Odin, the Allfather and chief of the gods, presided over Asgard, the realm of the gods. His son, Thor, the thunder god, wielded his mighty hammer, Mjölnir, to protect both gods and humans from the forces of chaos.

Frequent interactions with giants, dwarves, and other supernatural beings were common in Norse mythology. The world tree, Yggdrasil, connected the nine realms, including Midgard (Earth) and the land of the dead, Helheim. This complex cosmology reflects the deep reverence the Norse had for the natural world and its mysteries.

The Power of Runes

Norse superstitions were closely tied to the use of runes, the ancient script of the Norse people. Runes were believed to possess magical properties, and inscriptions could be found on everything from weapons to gravestones. The act of carving or writing runes was seen as a way to invoke the power of the gods and bring protection or fortune.

The Role of the Fylgja

In Norse belief, every individual had a fylgja, a supernatural guardian spirit often taking the form of an animal. This fylgja was believed to accompany a person throughout their life, and its well-being was closely tied to the individual's fate. To see one's own fylgja in dreams or visions was considered significant and could foretell one's destiny.

The Ties to Nature

The Norse people were deeply attuned to the rhythms of nature, and many superstitions revolved around natural phenomena. The Northern Lights, known as the "Borealis," were seen as a sign from the gods, a celestial display of their power. Lunar and solar eclipses were also viewed with awe and often interpreted as omens.

Tales of Elves and Trolls

Norse folklore is replete with tales of elves, light-dwelling beings, and trolls, dark and often malevolent creatures. These stories served as warnings and explanations for natural phenomena. Elves were associated with light and beauty, while trolls were creatures of darkness and chaos.

The Power of Seers and Shamans

Seers, known as völvas, were highly respected in Norse society. They were believed to possess the ability to see into the future, communicate with the spirits, and offer guidance to their communities. The völvas conducted rituals and sacrifices to gain insight and maintain harmony with the spirit world.

Superstitions in Daily Life

Superstitions were woven into the fabric of everyday life. It was considered bad luck to speak the name of certain creatures, like the wolf, as it was believed to summon their presence. To ward off evil, people often hung protective amulets, such as Thor's hammer, above doorways.

Transportation in Norway: From Ferries to Hurtigruten

Norway, a land of stunning natural beauty, is a country known for its efficient and varied transportation systems that enable both residents and visitors to explore its rugged landscapes and vibrant cities. From ferries that navigate its intricate network of fjords to the iconic Hurtigruten coastal voyage, Norway's transportation infrastructure is a testament to its commitment to accessibility and sustainability.

The Extensive Road Network

Norway boasts an extensive road network that connects its cities and towns, making road trips a popular mode of transportation. The country's highways are well-maintained and often wind through breathtaking scenery, from dramatic mountain passes to serene coastal routes. The E6, one of Norway's primary north-south routes, stretches from the southern tip of the country to its northernmost reaches, providing access to many regions along the way.

The Efficient Rail System

Norway's railway system is another vital component of its transportation network. The trains are known for their punctuality and comfort, offering passengers a scenic journey through the countryside. The Bergen Line, for example, connects Oslo and Bergen, traversing the stunning Hardangervidda plateau and offering panoramic views of lakes, waterfalls, and snow-capped peaks.

Ferries: Navigating the Fjords

In a country renowned for its fjords, ferries play a crucial role in connecting communities separated by waterways. These ferries provide not only transportation but also an opportunity to savor the natural beauty of Norway from the water. Iconic fjords like Geirangerfjord and Nærøyfjord are accessible by ferry, offering passengers unforgettable vistas of towering cliffs and cascading waterfalls.

Hurtigruten: The Coastal Express

No discussion of Norwegian transportation would be complete without mentioning Hurtigruten, often referred to as the "world's most beautiful voyage." This coastal express service has been a lifeline for many remote coastal communities for over a century. It offers a unique blend of transportation and exploration, with ships carrying passengers and cargo along the stunning Norwegian coastline. Travelers on Hurtigruten can witness the mesmerizing Northern Lights in the winter or the endless daylight of the Midnight Sun in the summer.

Air Travel and Domestic Flights

For those looking to cover vast distances quickly, Norway's domestic flights are a convenient option. The country has numerous airports, including major hubs in Oslo, Bergen, and Trondheim. Domestic flights make it easy to reach destinations in the northern reaches of Norway or explore the stunning Arctic archipelago of Svalbard.

Bicycling and Walking

In Norway, sustainable transportation is also encouraged. Many cities, including Oslo, have invested in extensive bicycle lanes, making cycling a popular and eco-friendly mode of transport. Additionally, Norway's cities are designed to be pedestrian-friendly, with well-maintained sidewalks and a focus on creating walkable urban spaces.

Norse Architecture: Stave Churches and Modern Designs

Norse architecture is a fascinating journey through time, reflecting the evolution of a culture deeply rooted in its natural surroundings and history. From the iconic stave churches that date back to the medieval era to the innovative and modern designs that shape Norway's contemporary skyline, this chapter explores the unique architectural heritage of this Nordic nation.

Stave Churches: A Glimpse into the Past

One of the most iconic and enduring symbols of Norse architecture is the stave church. These wooden structures, characterized by their vertical staves or posts, have a history dating back to the early Middle Ages. Stave churches are not only remarkable for their age but also for their intricate design and construction.

The Borgund Stave Church, built around 1180, is a prime example of this architectural style. Its distinctive dragon-head carvings and the interlocking wooden framework showcase the craftsmanship of the time. These churches, often adorned with Christian symbols and intricate carvings, have become cherished cultural and historical landmarks.

Viking Architecture: Simplicity and Functionality

During the Viking Age, Norse architecture emphasized functionality and adaptability. Viking longhouses were the primary residential structures, constructed using timber and thatch roofs. These longhouses accommodated both living quarters and areas for livestock, showcasing the pragmatic approach of the Vikings.

Medieval Influence: Stone Churches and Castles

As Norway transitioned from the Viking Age to the medieval period, stone structures began to emerge. Romanesque and Gothic influences gave rise to grand stone churches and fortifications. The Nidaros Cathedral in Trondheim is a prime example of this era's architectural splendor. Its soaring spires and intricate detailing reflect the importance of Christianity in medieval Norway.

Modern Marvels: Norwegian Contemporary Architecture

In the modern era, Norway's architectural landscape has seen a remarkable transformation. Norwegian architects have gained international recognition for their innovative and sustainable designs. Oslo, the capital, is home to iconic modern structures like the Oslo Opera House, which resembles an iceberg emerging from the fjord, and the striking Barcode Project, a collection of high-rise buildings that redefine the city's skyline.

Norway's commitment to sustainability is reflected in its contemporary architecture. The Powerhouse Kjørbo, for example, is one of the world's most energy-efficient office buildings, producing more energy than it consumes.

The Beauty of Blend: Traditional and Modern

What makes Norse architecture truly unique is its ability to blend the old with the new seamlessly. Many modern Norwegian buildings incorporate traditional elements, paying homage to the country's rich architectural heritage. The Holmenkollen Ski Jump, a stunning modern structure, stands atop the historic Holmenkollen hill, bridging the gap between past and present.

Norwegian Royals: A Modern Monarchy

The Norwegian monarchy is a testament to the country's rich history and its commitment to a constitutional and modern form of governance. Norway's royal family holds a special place in the hearts of its citizens, serving as both symbols of tradition and representatives of the nation's values.

A Constitutional Monarchy

Norway's monarchy is constitutional, meaning that the royal family's powers are largely ceremonial and symbolic. The King or Queen serves as the head of state, while the Prime Minister is the head of government. This system was established in the early 20th century when Norway gained independence from Sweden.

King Harald V: A Long Reign

King Harald V, the current monarch as of my knowledge cutoff date in 2022, ascended to the throne in 1991 and has played a crucial role in maintaining the stability and continuity of the Norwegian monarchy. His reign has spanned several decades, and he is known for his dedication to his role and his efforts to represent Norway both domestically and internationally.

Queen Sonja: A Beloved Consort

Queen Sonja, King Harald's wife, has been a beloved figure in Norway since her marriage to the King in 1968. She is known for her involvement in cultural and social causes and her support for the arts. Together with King Harald, they have represented Norway on state visits and engagements worldwide.

Crown Prince Haakon and Crown Princess Mette-Marit

Crown Prince Haakon, the heir apparent to the throne, is a figure who has garnered much attention and respect. His marriage to Crown Princess Mette-Marit in 2001 brought new energy to the monarchy. Crown Princess Mette-Marit, who had a previous life as a commoner, has been praised for her down-to-earth approach and her work on issues such as health and youth empowerment.

The Next Generation: Princess Ingrid Alexandra and Prince Sverre Magnus

The royal couple has two children, Princess Ingrid Alexandra and Prince Sverre Magnus. Ingrid Alexandra, as the eldest, is second in line to the throne after her father. The Norwegian monarchy, like many others in Europe, has embraced a system of gender-neutral succession, ensuring that the most qualified heir, regardless of gender, will inherit the throne.

Royal Duties and Representation

The Norwegian royal family plays an essential role in representing the nation at home and abroad. They attend state functions, welcome foreign dignitaries, and participate in cultural and charitable events. Their presence is a source of pride for many Norwegians, and they are often seen as unifying figures who transcend political divides.

Respect for Tradition and Adaptation to Modernity

What sets the Norwegian monarchy apart is its ability to respect tradition while adapting to the modern world. The royal family remains connected to the people through public appearances, and they are known for their humility and approachability.

Healthcare in Norway: A Comprehensive System

The healthcare system in Norway is often cited as a model of excellence, offering its citizens and residents a comprehensive and inclusive approach to healthcare. Rooted in principles of equality, accessibility, and high-quality care, the Norwegian healthcare system has consistently ranked among the top in the world. In this chapter, we will delve into the key aspects that make healthcare in Norway a noteworthy example of a well-functioning system.

Universal Healthcare Coverage

At the core of the Norwegian healthcare system is the principle of universal coverage. This means that every Norwegian citizen and legal resident has access to healthcare services, regardless of their socio-economic status or employment. The Norwegian government funds the system through taxes, ensuring that healthcare is both affordable and accessible to all.

Primary Healthcare: The First Point of Contact

The Norwegian healthcare system emphasizes the importance of primary care as the initial point of contact for patients. General practitioners (GPs) play a central role in providing basic healthcare services, including diagnosis, treatment, and referrals to specialists if needed. Patients can freely choose their GP, ensuring a level of personalization in their healthcare.

Specialized Care: World-Class Hospitals

Norway boasts a network of modern and well-equipped hospitals and specialized healthcare facilities. These institutions provide a wide range of medical services, including surgeries, cancer treatments, and advanced diagnostics. Notably, Norway has consistently ranked high in healthcare quality indicators, with low mortality rates and high life expectancies.

Patient Choice and Involvement

Patient autonomy is a key principle in Norwegian healthcare. Patients have the right to be involved in decisions regarding their treatment, and healthcare professionals encourage active participation in healthcare choices. This approach fosters a sense of ownership over one's health and treatment plan.

Elderly Care: A Growing Priority

As the Norwegian population ages, elderly care has become a priority. The government has implemented various programs and initiatives to support the elderly, including home care services and nursing homes. Ensuring a high quality of life for senior citizens is a fundamental aspect of Norway's healthcare system.

Mental Health and Well-being

Norway places a strong emphasis on mental health and well-being. Access to mental health services is readily available, and efforts are made to reduce stigma surrounding mental health issues. Various support programs and therapies are offered to those in need, ensuring that mental health is treated with the same level of importance as physical health.

Emergency Services: Rapid Response

Norway's emergency medical services are known for their rapid response times and high level of competence. Whether it's a medical emergency or an accident, the healthcare system is designed to provide timely and effective care.

Challenges and Future Directions

While Norway's healthcare system is commendable, it also faces challenges, such as rising healthcare costs due to an aging population. Nonetheless, the government continually evaluates and adapts the system to meet evolving needs and maintain its high standard of care.

In conclusion, healthcare in Norway is a comprehensive and inclusive system that embodies the principles of equality and accessibility. It ensures that every citizen and resident can access high-quality healthcare services without financial barriers. With a strong focus on primary care, specialized services, patient involvement, and well-being, Norway's healthcare system stands as a model for nations striving to provide excellent healthcare to their populations.

Norwegian Innovation and Technology

In the realm of innovation and technology, Norway has made significant strides, showcasing a commitment to excellence and sustainability. This chapter explores the country's achievements, innovations, and technological advancements that have not only enhanced the lives of its citizens but also made an impact on the global stage.

Green Tech and Renewable Energy

One of Norway's most notable contributions to the world is its prowess in renewable energy. The country harnesses its natural resources, particularly hydroelectric power, to generate clean and sustainable energy. The vast network of fjords provides ideal conditions for hydropower production, making Norway one of the largest producers of hydroelectricity in Europe.

Furthermore, Norway has invested heavily in wind and solar energy, with innovative projects aimed at reducing carbon emissions and combating climate change. The nation's dedication to green technology extends beyond its borders, as it actively participates in international efforts to promote renewable energy solutions.

Electric Mobility

Norway has been at the forefront of electric mobility, becoming a global leader in electric vehicle (EV) adoption. Government incentives, such as tax breaks and toll exemptions, have made EVs an attractive option for Norwegians. This has led to a surge in electric vehicle sales, with Norway boasting one of the highest rates of EV ownership per capita in the world.

Maritime Innovation

Given its rich maritime history and extensive coastline, Norway has a deep connection to the sea. The country has pioneered advancements in maritime technology, particularly in the field of shipping and offshore industries. Norwegian companies are renowned for their expertise in building safe and efficient vessels, and the nation's maritime sector is a key player in global shipping.

Space Exploration

Norway may not be a space superpower, but it has made significant contributions to space exploration and satellite technology. The country has launched several successful satellites, contributing to telecommunications, Earth observation, and scientific research. Norwegian scientists and engineers continue to collaborate with international space agencies, pushing the boundaries of space science.

Innovation Ecosystem

Norway's innovation ecosystem is robust, with a strong emphasis on research and development (R&D). The government, in partnership with private enterprises, invests heavily in R&D activities across various sectors, including healthcare, technology, and renewable energy. This investment has led to groundbreaking discoveries and innovations.

Education and Research

Norwegian universities and research institutions are globally recognized for their excellence. The country fosters a culture of curiosity and exploration, nurturing talent in fields such as science, engineering, and technology. Many Norwegian scientists and researchers have made significant contributions to their respective fields on an international scale.

Start-up Culture

Norway's start-up scene is flourishing, with numerous innovative companies emerging in recent years. The government provides support and resources for entrepreneurs, enabling them to turn their ideas into successful businesses. Many of these start-ups focus on technology and sustainability, aligning with Norway's commitment to a greener future.

In conclusion, Norway's journey in innovation and technology is a testament to its dedication to sustainable development and progress. From renewable energy to electric mobility and space exploration, the country has consistently demonstrated its ability to adapt and thrive in an ever-evolving technological landscape. Norway's contributions to innovation not only benefit its citizens but also have a global impact, shaping a brighter and more sustainable future for all.

Planning Your Trip to Norway: Tips and Resources

Embarking on a journey to Norway is an exciting prospect, as this Nordic wonderland offers a multitude of experiences for travelers. Whether you're drawn to the breathtaking landscapes, rich cultural heritage, or innovative cities, Norway has something to offer every type of explorer. To ensure your trip is as smooth and enjoyable as possible, here are some essential tips and resources to help you plan your adventure.

Visa Requirements

Before packing your bags, it's crucial to check Norway's visa requirements. Norway is part of the Schengen Area, which means that if you're a citizen of a Schengen Agreement country, you can enter Norway without a visa for short stays. However, it's essential to verify the specific entry requirements based on your nationality and the purpose of your visit.

Travel Insurance

Travel insurance is a must when visiting Norway. It provides coverage for unexpected events, such as medical emergencies, trip cancellations, and lost luggage. Be sure to purchase comprehensive travel insurance to protect yourself during your journey.

Currency

The official currency of Norway is the Norwegian Krone (NOK). While credit and debit cards are widely accepted, it's a good idea to carry some cash for small purchases and emergencies. ATMs are readily available throughout the country, making it easy to withdraw local currency.

Language

The official languages of Norway are Norwegian, specifically Bokmål and Nynorsk. While many Norwegians speak English fluently, especially in urban areas and tourist destinations, learning a few basic Norwegian phrases can enhance your travel experience and help you connect with locals.

Climate and Packing

Norway's climate varies from region to region and changes with the seasons. Coastal areas experience milder winters, while inland regions can have cold, snowy winters. Summers are generally mild and pleasant. Pack accordingly, taking into account the specific time of year and the regions you plan to visit. Layers are key to staying comfortable in Norway's ever-changing weather.

Transportation

Norway has an efficient and extensive transportation network, including trains, buses, and ferries. The country's rail system is known for its scenic routes, and traveling by train can be a memorable part of your journey. Consider purchasing an Oslo Pass or similar city passes if you plan to explore urban areas, as they often include public transportation and admission to attractions.

Accommodation

Norway offers a wide range of accommodation options, from luxurious hotels to budget-friendly hostels and cozy cabins. It's advisable to book your accommodations in advance, especially during the peak tourist season in the summer. Popular cities like Oslo, Bergen, and Tromsø can have high demand for lodging.

Activities and Attractions

Research and plan your activities and attractions ahead of time to make the most of your trip. Norway boasts a diverse range of experiences, from hiking in the fjords and witnessing the Northern Lights to exploring historic sites and sampling traditional cuisine. Consider guided tours or excursions to gain insights into the local culture and natural wonders.

Local Cuisine

Norwegian cuisine reflects the country's rich maritime heritage and natural resources. Be sure to savor local delicacies like freshly caught seafood, reindeer dishes, and traditional baked goods. Additionally, don't miss the opportunity to try aquavit, a popular Scandinavian spirit.

Respect Local Customs

Norwegians are known for their friendliness and politeness. It's customary to greet people with a smile and a nod when passing on hiking trails or in more remote areas. Tipping is not obligatory but appreciated, and 10% is the standard in restaurants. Always follow local customs and guidelines, such as taking off your shoes when entering someone's home.

Safety

Norway is generally a safe destination for travelers. However, it's essential to exercise standard safety precautions, such as safeguarding your belongings and being aware of your surroundings. In case of emergencies, Norway's emergency services can be reached by dialing 112.

By keeping these tips in mind and utilizing the available resources, you can plan a memorable and enjoyable trip to Norway. Whether you're a nature enthusiast, a history buff, or simply seeking adventure, Norway's beauty and culture await your exploration.

Epilogue

As we reach the conclusion of our journey through the fascinating tapestry of Norway, it's worth reflecting on the incredible depth and diversity this Nordic nation offers to those who explore its landscapes, culture, and history.

Throughout the preceding chapters, we've delved into the ancient past of Norway, from the icy grip of the Ice Age to the sagas of the Viking Age. We've explored the rise and fall of kingdoms, the union with Denmark, and the arduous path to independence in the 19th century. We've witnessed the emergence of modern Norway as a thriving nation, known for its innovation and social welfare system.

We've ventured into the realms of Norse mythology, the rich traditions of the Sami people, and the wonders of Norwegian wildlife and cuisine. We've marveled at the architectural beauty of stave churches and modern designs, and we've glimpsed into the lives of the Norwegian royals.

From the celestial phenomenon of the Northern Lights to the masterpieces of nature that are the Norwegian fjords, we've embraced the natural wonders of this land. We've wandered through vibrant cities like Oslo, Bergen, and Trondheim, each with its unique charm and history.

We've explored the Arctic city of Tromsø and the coastal gem of Kristiansand. We've admired the art nouveau beauty of Ålesund and ventured on a railway adventure in Narvik. We've strolled through the city of roses, Molde, and soaked in the maritime heritage of Bergen.

In the historical heartland of Trondheim, we've discovered the gateway to the Arctic in Tromsø. We've experienced Stavanger as an oil capital and cultural hub, and we've appreciated the coastal gem of Kristiansand.

We've learned about preserving traditions in Sami culture, and we've marveled at the natural wonderland of Norwegian wildlife. We've indulged in the flavors of Norwegian cuisine, from salmon to koldtbord. We've admired the functionality and beauty of Scandinavian design, and we've gazed upon the celestial phenomenon of the Northern Lights.

We've gained insights into Norwegian folklore and superstitions, danced to folk music, and explored the world of Norwegian literature. We've celebrated contemporary Norwegian art and artists and embraced the religious diversity that exists in Norway.

From Christmas traditions to holidays and festivals, we've glimpsed into the vibrant cultural tapestry of this nation. We've embarked on outdoor adventures, from hiking to skiing, and experienced the thrill of exploration.

We've touched upon the Norwegian language, offering tips for language enthusiasts, and we've journeyed through the comprehensive Norwegian education system. We've explored the principles of the Norwegian welfare state, characterized by social equality, and delved into sustainability and conservation efforts.

Innovation and technology have played a significant role in shaping modern Norway, and we've highlighted the remarkable achievements in this field. We've offered practical tips and resources for planning your trip, ensuring that your Norwegian adventure is both enjoyable and memorable.

As our journey through Norway concludes, it's important to remember that the beauty of this nation extends far beyond its stunning landscapes. It resides in the warmth of its people, the preservation of its traditions, and the spirit of innovation that drives it forward.

Norway's story is one of resilience, progress, and an unwavering connection to its natural surroundings. Whether you're an intrepid traveler, a culture enthusiast, or simply someone seeking to expand their horizons, Norway welcomes you with open arms and a wealth of experiences waiting to be discovered.

So, as you set forth on your own Norwegian adventure, remember the tales you've encountered in these pages and let them be your guide as you explore the land of the Vikings, a land where history meets modernity, where nature reigns supreme, and where the spirit of discovery knows no bounds.

Made in the USA
Las Vegas, NV
21 December 2024

14970787R00072